Property of Devereux

First Atlas

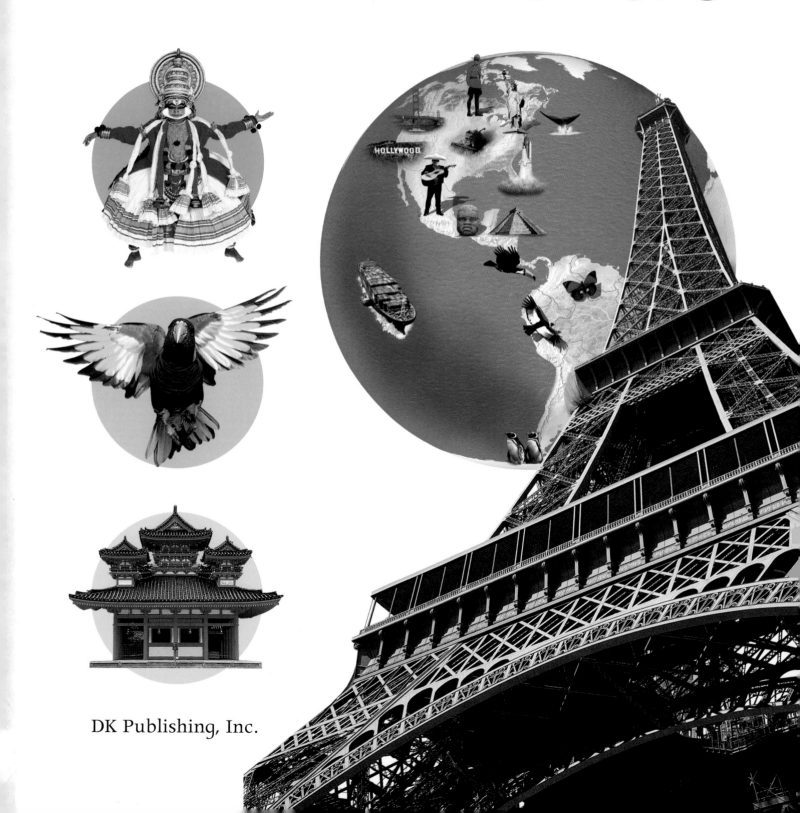

DK Publishing, Inc.

DK

LONDON, NEW YORK, MUNICH,
MELBOURNE, and DELHI

Authors Anita Ganeri and Chris Oxlade
Project senior editor Ben Morgan
Project senior art editor Janet Allis
Editor Simon Holland
Senior art editor Cheryl Telfer
Additional design Jacqueline Gooden,
Mary Sandberg, Floyd Sayer, Sonia Whillock
Editorial assistant Fleur Star
Digital map illustrator Peter Bull

Publishing manager Sue Leonard
Managing art editor Clare Shedden
US editor Christine Heilman
Jacket design Poppy Jenkins, Bob Warner
Picture researchers Martin Copeland,
Sean Hunter, Sarah Stewart-Richardson
Production controller Linda Dare
DTP designer Almudena Díaz

First American Edition, 2003

Published in the United States by
DK Publishing, Inc.
345 Hudson Street
New York, New York 10014

13 12 11 10 9 8 7 6 5
019-DD041-May/04

A Cataloging-in-Publication record for this book
is available from the Library of Congress.

ISBN 978-0-7566-0231-4

Color reproduction by Colourscan, Singapore
Printed in Hong Kong

Discover more at
www.dk.com

Contents

Our world

The top of the world

The Americas

Our world

Land covers a third of planet Earth, and water and ice cover the rest. We divide the land into seven main chunks called continents. The sea is divided into five major areas called oceans.

North America

Pacific Ocean

Atlantic Ocean

Inside the Earth

The inside of Earth is made of hot, molten rock that slowly swirls around like thick molasses. We live on a thin, solid crust, a bit like the crust of a pie.

South America

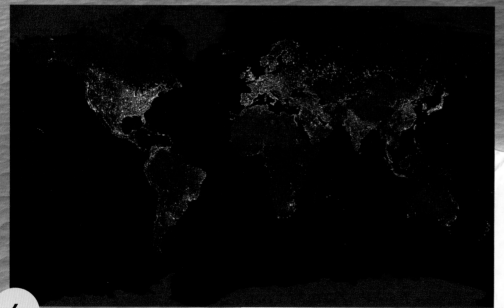

Where people live

This picture of Earth at night was taken by a satellite in space. The bright parts are made by lights on the surface. They show where the world's big cities and towns are.

How long would a trip around the equator take at walking speed?

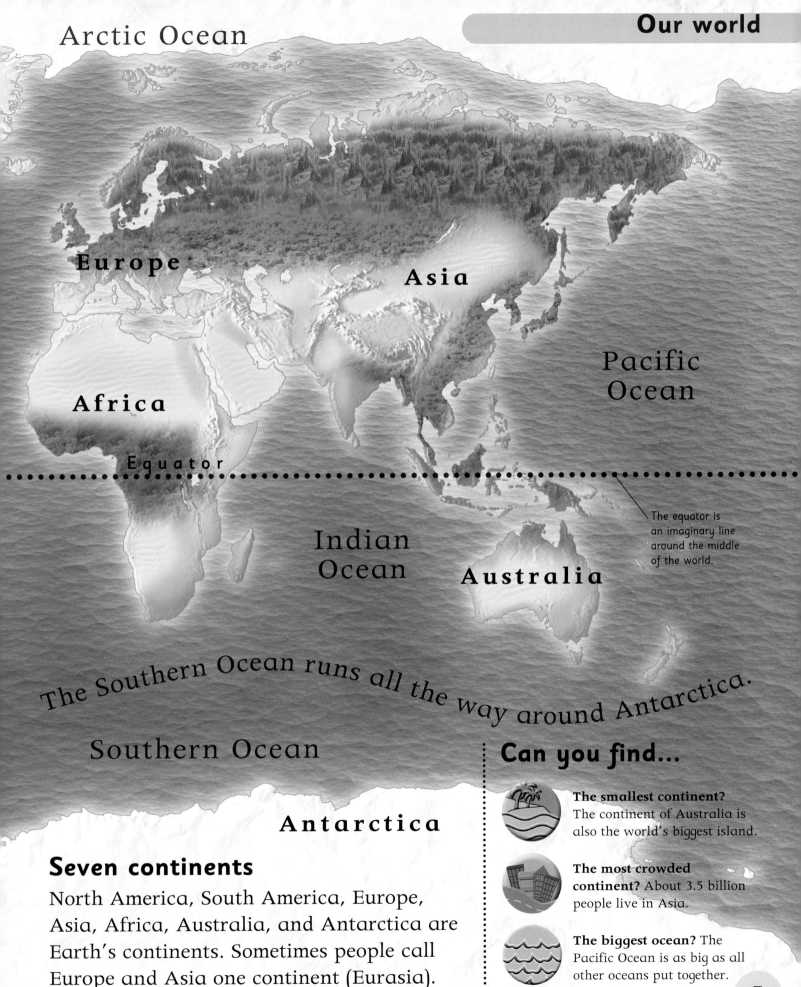

Arctic Ocean

Europe

Asia

Pacific Ocean

Africa

Equator

The equator is an imaginary line around the middle of the world.

Indian Ocean

Australia

The Southern Ocean runs all the way around Antarctica.

Southern Ocean

Antarctica

Seven continents

North America, South America, Europe, Asia, Africa, Australia, and Antarctica are Earth's continents. Sometimes people call Europe and Asia one continent (Eurasia).

Can you find...

The smallest continent? The continent of Australia is also the world's biggest island.

The most crowded continent? About 3.5 billion people live in Asia.

The biggest ocean? The Pacific Ocean is as big as all other oceans put together.

About a year (without stopping for a rest).

Maps and atlases

A map is a drawing of the ground that shows where towns, rivers, and other important features lie. An atlas is a book of maps.

Making a flat map of the world is like peeling an orange.

Thin areas need to be stretched to make a full rectangle.

Peeling the Earth
Earth is ball-shaped, so a globe is the best kind of map to show the whole planet. On a flat map, some areas are stretched or squashed.

How to use this book
This atlas is divided into map pages and information pages. The key tells you what the map symbols mean.

Key to maps

- ◉ CAPITAL CITY
- ● State capital
- • Town
- ▲ Mountain
- ••• Key feature
- ⌒ Border
- - - - State border
- ∿ River

Compass points show you which way is north, south, east, and west.

Small pictures show the things you might see if you visited the country, from famous buildings to native animals and national sports.

Atlas questions test your general knowledge about different parts of the world. The answer is upside down on the opposite page.

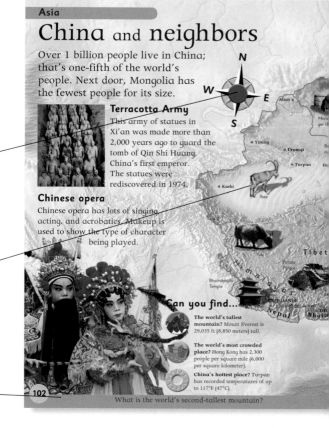

Asia
China and neighbors
Over 1 billion people live in China; that's one-fifth of the world's people. Next door, Mongolia has the fewest people for its size.

Terracotta Army
This army of statues in Xi'an was made more than 2,000 years ago to guard the tomb of Qin Shi Huang, China's first emperor. The statues were rediscovered in 1974.

Chinese opera
Chinese opera has lots of singing, acting, and acrobatics. Makeup is used to show the type of character being played.

Can you find...
The world's tallest mountain? Mount Everest is 29,035 ft (8,850 meters) tall.

The world's most crowded place? Hong Kong has 2,300 people per square mile (6,000 per square kilometer).

China's hottest place? Turpan has recorded temperatures of up to 117°F (47°C).

102

What is the world's second-tallest mountain?

Earth's landscapes
The background patterns on the maps show what the landscape and countryside are like in different parts of the world.

Deciduous forest
Forests of trees that lose their leaves in autumn.

Grassland
Flat, grassy plains with a few trees dotted around.

Coniferous forest
Forests of conifer trees, which stay green all year.

What kind of map shows just countries and their borders?

Types of maps

People use different kinds of maps for different purposes. Road maps help drivers find their way. In cities, people on foot use street maps.

Road maps show routes between towns and cities.

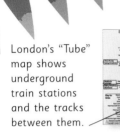

London's "Tube" map shows underground train stations and the tracks between them.

A street map shows city streets and buildings.

get going
To find out why world maps are stretched, peel an orange and see if you can make a rectangle with the skin. Does it help if you cut the skin into thin strips?

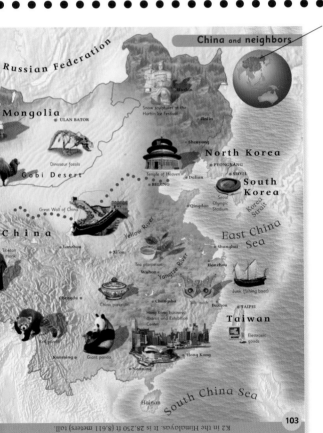

Globes show where the map is on Earth's surface. The featured countries are highlighted in red.

Buttons contain a file of facts about special topics, such as local animals or foods.

Information pages

After each map are information pages, which are packed with amazing facts about the countries in the map.

Get going circles contain great ideas for projects and experiments you can carry out.

Desert
Dry sand and rock with hardly any plants.

Rainforest
A jungle of tall trees and layers of thick undergrowth.

Snow and ice
High in the mountains and near the poles.

Mountains
Rugged landscape of tall hills and valleys, often snow-covered.

Oceans
Seas and oceans cover two-thirds of the Earth.

A political map.

World climates

Near the Earth's poles, it is freezing cold all year. But near the equator it is always hot and rainy. We say that the poles and the equator have different climates.

Arctic Circle

Tropic of Cancer

Equator

Tropic of Capricorn

Antarctic Circle

Between the Arctic Circle and the Tropic of Cancer, the climate is temperate.

Between the two tropics, the climate is tropical.

Inside the Arctic and Antarctic circles, the climate is polar.

Climate zones

World maps show horizontal lines that divide Earth into zones with different climates. Tropical zones are always warm and polar zones are always cold. Temperate zones are a mixture of the two, with warm summers and cool winters.

Polar climate

Antarctica has a polar climate. It is always freezing cold, and there are fierce blizzards. Penguins keep warm by growing a thick layer of fat and huddling together.

Conifer forest

In some parts of the temperate zones, winters are long and cold, so conifers are the only trees that survive. Some flowers appear in the short summers.

Emperor penguins

What's another name for tropical grassland?

Desert
A desert climate is very dry all year. Deserts can be baking hot in the day but very cold at night.

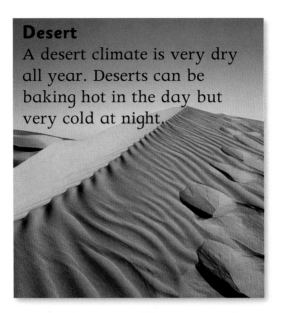

Toucans live in tropical rainforest. They have huge beaks for eating tropical fruits.

Tropical forest
Places near the equator are both warm and rainy all year. Dense tropical rainforests grow here.

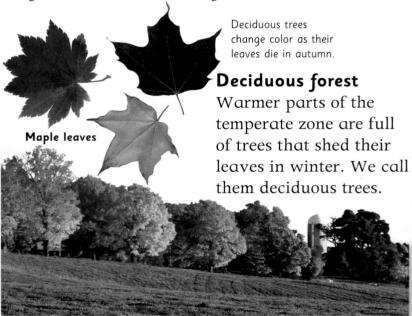

Tropical grassland
Some tropical places have a dry season and a rainy season every year. Trees are less common here, and the ground is covered with grass.

Deciduous trees change color as their leaves die in autumn.

Deciduous forest
Warmer parts of the temperate zone are full of trees that shed their leaves in winter. We call them deciduous trees.

Maple leaves

Poison dart frog

Savanna

Seas and oceans

Seas and oceans cover about two-thirds of the world. Beneath the surface, they are full of life. Most sea creatures live in habitats near the coast, such as coral reefs. But there is also life far out in the open ocean and on the deep sea floor.

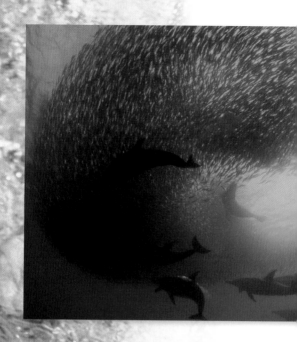

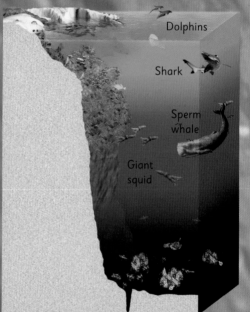

Dolphins

Shark

Sperm whale

Giant squid

Most animals and plants live in the sunlit surface waters near the coast.

Deeper down, the water is cold and gloomy.

No light reaches the deep sea. It is pitch black here.

Under the sea

Away from the shore, the land slopes steeply into the sea. Some of the seabed is covered in flat plains, but there are also mountains and valleys.

Ocean waves

Waves are caused by wind blowing across the sea. When they reach shallow water, they tumble over and turn into breakers.

Animals of the deep

Some very strange animals live in the deep sea. The gulper eel lives 4 miles (7 km) down and catches dead creatures as they sink from above. Its mouth is so huge it can swallow animals bigger than itself.

What is the deepest place in the world's oceans?

The open ocean

Out in the open ocean, there is less life than near the coast. Occasional shoals of fish are food for big animals, such as dolphins.

Dolphins sometimes drive fish into tight balls before attacking them.

Kelp forests

This seaweed is called giant kelp. It grows from the seabed, making thick forests where fish and other animals live.

Angelfish

Life on the coast

Animals and plants that live on the shore are battered by the waves. They cling to rocks or burrow into sandy beaches.

Tentacle of a sea cucumber (an animal related to a starfish).

Coral reefs

Coral reefs are home to thousands of different sea creatures, including many colorful fish. Reefs grow slowly in shallow tropical seas and are made up of the hard cases of tiny animals (corals).

The Mariana Trench in the Pacific Ocean. It is 6.9 miles (11 km) deep.

The Arctic

At the top of the world is the North Pole, and around this is an area called the Arctic. The Arctic is mostly ocean. In its center is a gigantic lump of floating ice that never completely melts. Farther out are the northern tips of the continents and the huge island of Greenland.

Arctic people

Arctic people live in the icy lands around the Arctic Ocean. The weather is too cold for growing crops, so Arctic people get all their food from animals. They survive by fishing, herding reindeer, and hunting seals and whales.

An imaginary line called the Arctic Circle marks the outer edge of the Arctic region.

Alaska

Prudhoe Ba

Beaufort Sea

Moose

Arctic tern

Canada

Queen Elizabeth Islands

Ellesmere Island

Ptarmigan

•Thule

Polar bear

Greenland

Who was the first person to reach the North Pole?

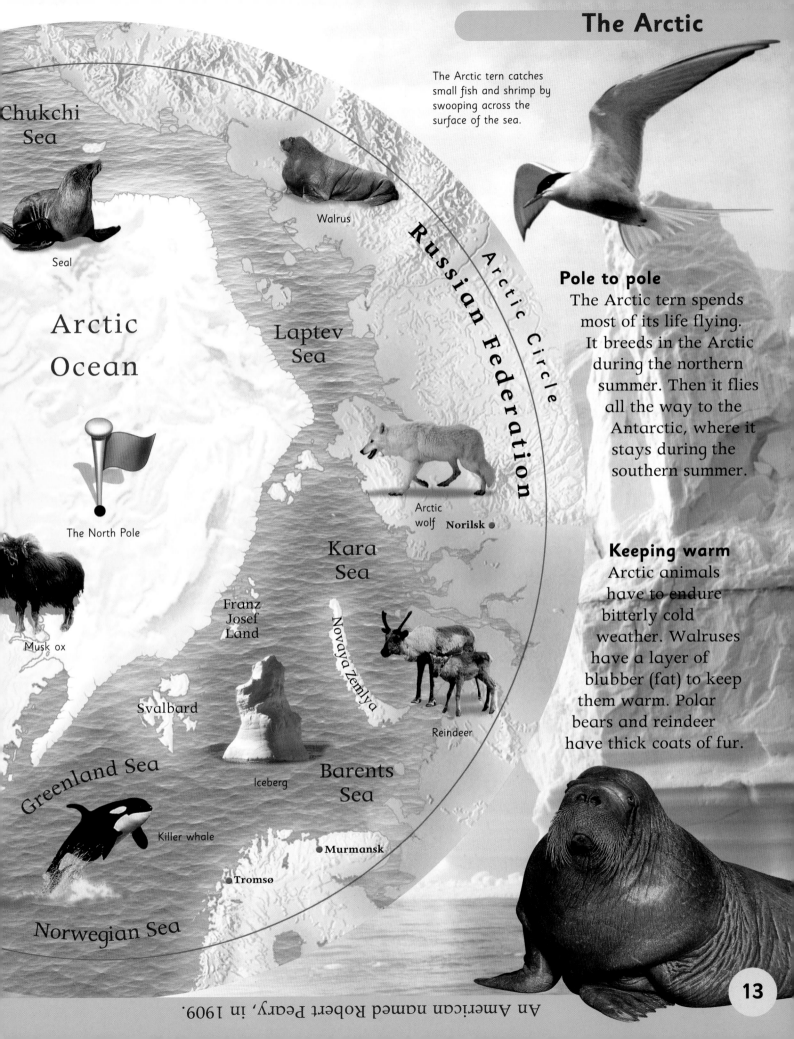

Chukchi
Sea

Seal

Walrus

The Arctic tern catches small fish and shrimp by swooping across the surface of the sea.

Arctic
Ocean

Russian Federation

Arctic Circle

The North Pole

Laptev
Sea

Arctic
wolf **Norilsk**

Musk ox

Kara
Sea

Franz
Josef
Land

Novaya Zemlya

Reindeer

Svalbard

Iceberg

Greenland Sea

Barents
Sea

Killer whale

Murmansk

Tromsø

Norwegian Sea

Pole to pole

The Arctic tern spends most of its life flying. It breeds in the Arctic during the northern summer. Then it flies all the way to the Antarctic, where it stays during the southern summer.

Keeping warm

Arctic animals have to endure bitterly cold weather. Walruses have a layer of blubber (fat) to keep them warm. Polar bears and reindeer have thick coats of fur.

An American named Robert Peary, in 1909.

13

The Arctic

The Arctic is a magical place, but it is also freezing cold and dangerous. For the people and animals that live there, life is very tough.

Arctic travel

Arctic people have to travel across ice, snow, and the sea.

Snowshoes spread your weight to stop your feet from sinking into snow.

Snowmobiles zoom over snow on motorized treads and steerable skis.

Kayaks are wooden canoes used by Inuit people for fishing.

Sleds carry heavy loads or people. They are pulled by dogs.

Northern lights

At night, the Arctic sky lights up with shimmering colors called the northern lights. They are caused by particles from space hitting Earth's atmosphere.

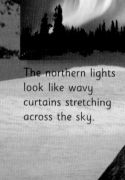

The northern lights look like wavy curtains stretching across the sky.

Thick fur clothes and fur-lined hoods keep out the cold.

Rifles are used for hunting and to scare away polar bears.

Inuit hunters

The Inuit people live in Canada and Greenland. They use spears and guns to hunt seals, whales, fish, walruses, and polar bears.

Why is summer in the Arctic unusual?

Polar bear
The world's biggest and most deadly kind of bear is the polar bear, which lives in the Arctic. Polar bears mostly hunt seals, but they occasionally kill people, too.

Igloos
Most Inuit people live in modern houses in small towns. On long hunting trips they sleep in igloos—temporary shelters made from blocks of snow.

Icebreakers
In winter the Arctic Ocean freezes solid. Special ships called icebreakers keep channels clear.

Husky dogs
Arctic people use teams of husky dogs to pull sleds. Huskies originally come from Siberia. They are very strong and have thicker fur than most dogs.

15

The Sun doesn't set.

Canada and Alaska

Canada is the second-largest country in the world, and Alaska is the largest of all the US states. Despite their huge size, both places have small populations, because much of the land is covered in thick forest or frozen for most of the year.

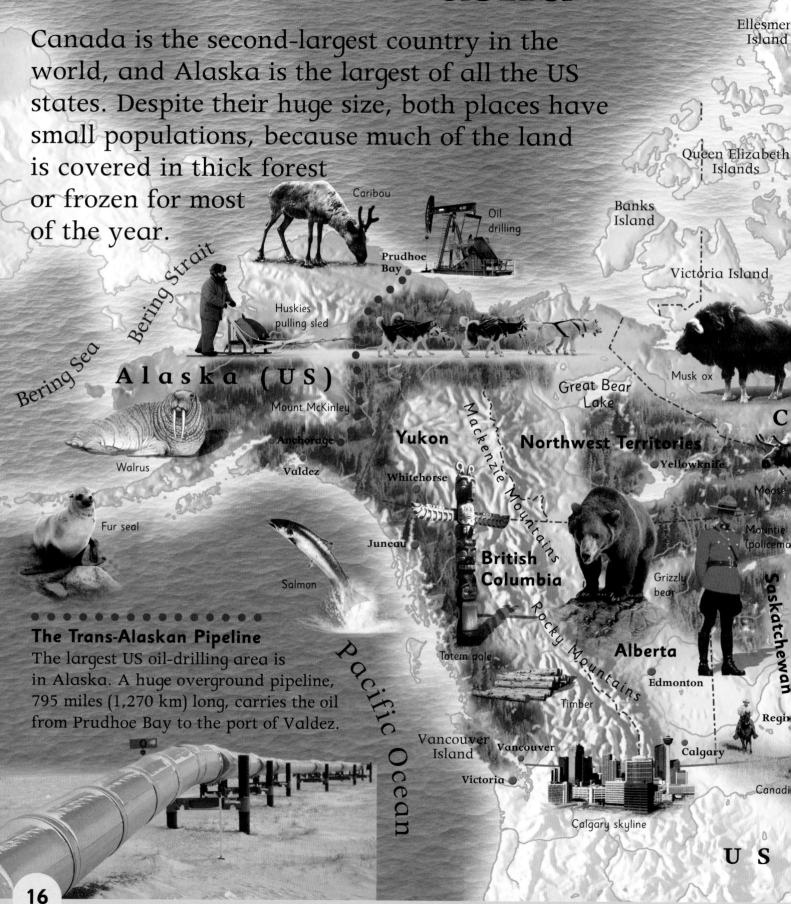

Caribou

Oil drilling

Prudhoe Bay

Huskies pulling sled

Bering Strait

Bering Sea

Alaska (US)

Walrus

Mount McKinley

Anchorage

Valdez

Yukon

Whitehorse

Juneau

Fur seal

Salmon

Ellesmere Island

Queen Elizabeth Islands

Banks Island

Victoria Island

Musk ox

Great Bear Lake

Northwest Territories

Yellowknife

Mackenzie Mountains

Moose

Grizzly bear

Mountie (policeman)

British Columbia

Rocky Mountains

Alberta

Edmonton

Timber

Saskatchewan

Totem pole

Regina

The Trans-Alaskan Pipeline
The largest US oil-drilling area is in Alaska. A huge overground pipeline, 795 miles (1,270 km) long, carries the oil from Prudhoe Bay to the port of Valdez.

Pacific Ocean

Vancouver Island

Vancouver

Victoria

Calgary

Canadi

Calgary skyline

U S

What is the tallest mountain in North America, at 20,320 ft (6,194 m) high?

Industries

Here are some of the main industries in the region.

Timber from trees is used as building material or for making furniture.

Oil is used to make fuels like gasoline and chemicals such as plastics.

Wheat is grown in the center of Canada on prairies, which are huge, flat fields.

Metals such as zinc, aluminum, gold, and silver are mined in Canada.

N
E
W
S

Hooded seal

Baffin Island

Inuit children

Nunavut

Canada goose

Iqaluit

Right whales (whale-watching is a popular activity)

a n a d a

Black bear

Newfoundland and Labrador

Newfoundland dog

St. John's

Hudson Bay

Beluga whale and calf

Mining

Quebec

Gannet

Prince Edward Island

New Brunswick

Charlottetown

Nova Scotia

Halifax

Fredericton

Quebec

Maple leaf

Beaver

Snowboarding

CN Tower Toronto

Montreal

OTTAWA

Manitoba **Ontario**

Lake Superior

Lake Huron

Lake Michigan

Lake Erie

Toronto

Lake Ontario

Niagara Falls

Winnipeg

airies

Atlantic Ocean

Harbor porpoises

Mount McKinley (Denali).

17

Canada and Alaska

Magnificent scenery and unspoiled wilderness make Canada and Alaska great places to live. However, the winters are long, dark, and bitterly cold. Most people live in the south, where the weather is mildest.

Alaskan landscape

The ten tallest mountains in the US are all in Alaska. Mount McKinley (Denali) is the highest. Surrounding these huge mountains are forests and lakes.

Animal life

Despite the chilly weather, Canada, Alaska, and the surrounding sea are home to some spectacular animals.

Husky dogs are used to pull sleds that transport people and materials.

Walruses group together on Arctic beaches or floating sheets of ice.

Moose live in woods close to swamps, lakes, and other watery areas.

Right whales are sometimes hit by ships because they swim slowly.

Fur seals grow to about 7 ft (2 m) long. They eat fish and some birds.

Logging industry

Canada's trees can grow to enormous sizes, especially along the rainy west coast. Lumberjacks cut them down for lumber (wood), which is used for building houses and making furniture.

What could you put on your pancakes to sweeten them?

Totem pole

Hockey

Thanks to the cold winters, Canadians can play hockey on outdoor rinks or frozen lakes and ponds. Hockey is the world's fastest team sport.

Native peoples

The Kwakiutl and Haida Indians were among the first people to live on Canada's west coast. They carved totem poles to tell stories about their families and traditions.

French Canadians

Europeans started coming to Canada in the 17th century, and many came from France. Today, most French Canadians live in the region called Quebec.

Hotel Chateau Frontenac, Quebec City, Quebec, Canada

Sweet treat

Maple syrup is made from the sap of maple trees. To make it, you drill a hole in a tree, collect the sap that dribbles out, and boil it until it thickens. Sugar maple trees produce the sweetest sap.

CN Tower, Toronto

This is the world's tallest tower (but not the tallest building, since buildings have floors). It is 1,814 ft (553 m) high, which is taller than 300 people standing on each other's heads. A glass elevator goes up the outside to the main deck, which has a revolving restaurant and a scary glass floor.

Maple syrup.

United States of America

The United States of America is an enormous country made up of 50 states. There are mountains, deserts, forests, wetlands, and vast plains in the US.

Technology industry

Seattle

Olympia

Washington

Columbia River

Salem

Oregon

Grizzly bear (brown bear)

Helena

Montana

Bison   Missou

Mount Rushmore National Memorial

Skiing in the Rockies

Rocky

Boise

Idaho

Mountains

Great Salt Lake

Wyoming

Golden Gate Bridge

Cheyenne

Wheat harvestin

Carson City

Mountain lion

Salt Lake City

Nevada

Utah

Denver

Colorado

San Francisco

Pacific Ocean

California

HOLLYWOOD

Hollywood Hills

Los Angeles

Death Valley National Monument

Monument Valley

Colorado River

Arizona

Sonoran

Desert

Phoenix

Santa Fe

New Mexico

Road-runner

Socorro space telescope

Gila monster

Rio Grande

Hawaii

One of the 50 US states is a group of eight volcanic islands in the Pacific Ocean. This state is called Hawaii.

Kauai

Niihau   **Honolulu**

Oahu   Molokai

Lanai   Maui

Hawaii

Mount Kilauea, on the main island of Hawaii, is the world's most active volcano.

N

W   E

S

Mexico

Which is the only US state not shown on this map?

Canada

This map shows 48 of the 50 states of the US. The other two states are thousands of miles away. Alaska is northwest of Canada, and Hawaii is in the middle of the Pacific Ocean.

Lake Superior

Lake Huron

Lake Ontario

Blueberries

Augusta

Maine

Bismarck

North Dakota

Minnesota

Wisconsin

Lake Michigan

Michigan

Vermont

New Hampshire

New York

Massachusetts

Boston

Rhode Island

Connecticut

Dairy farming

Detroit

Lake Erie

Pennsylvania

Harrisburg

Statue of Liberty

New York

New Jersey

Pierre

South Dakota

Iowa

Chicago

Indiana

Ohio

Delaware

Maryland

Nebraska

Football

WASHINGTON, DC

West Virginia

Virginia

The Capitol building, Washington, DC

Lincoln

Raccoon

Sears Tower, Chicago

Illinois

St. Louis

Ohio River

Topeka

Missouri

American bald eagle

Kentucky

Raleigh

North Carolina

Kansas

Great Plains

Tennessee

Appalachian Mountains

South Carolina

Oklahoma City

"Tornado Alley"

Arkansas

Little Rock

Country music

Mississippi

Atlanta

Oklahoma

Dallas

Mississippi River

Alabama

Georgia

Montgomery

Kennedy Space Center

Oil wells

Texas

Paddle steamer

Louisiana

Baton Rouge

Tallahassee

Florida

Jazz music

New Orleans

The Everglades

Dolphin-watching

Cowboy

Gulf of Mexico

American alligator

Miami

Atlantic Ocean

Alaska (see page 18).

United States of America

The US is the world's richest and most powerful country. Many of the people live in huge, modern cities, yet there are still vast areas of unspoiled natural wilderness.

Santa Monica pier and beach, California

The Pacific Coast

The southwest coast of the US has warm, sunny weather and great beaches. Surfers come here for the huge waves, and roller-bladers skate up and down the beachfront.

Visitors climb 354 steps to reach the statue's crown.

New York City

With nearly 8 million inhabitants, New York City is the biggest city in the US. Its most famous landmark is the Statue of Liberty in the harbor. It is 305 ft (92 m) tall and made of copper.

These towers of rock are

What is the hottest place in the US?

Hawaii

The Hawaiian islands are the tops of volcanoes in the Pacific Ocean. Mount Kilauea has been erupting for years. Its lava flows into the sea and makes huge clouds of steam.

The Mississippi River

The Mississippi is North America's longest river. Barges carry cargo like oil, coal, and steel along it. Here the Mississippi is flowing past the Gateway Arch in St. Louis, Missouri.

American alligator

Swamps and alligators

There are huge grassy swamps called the Everglades in the state of Florida. The swamps are home to all kinds of wild animals, including alligators, panthers, and turtles.

the crumbling remains of ancient mountains.

Deserts and canyons

The southwestern US is hot and dry. There are spectacular rocky towers called mesas, cactus-filled deserts, and deep canyons.

get going

Make an American flag like the one in the back of this book. Draw 7 red stripes on a sheet of paper, but leave a corner blank. Color the corner blue and stick 50 small small white stars on it.

Death Valley, California.

Life in the US

The US is one of the world's most diverse countries. Most Americans are descended from people who moved here from other countries.

The Capitol building, Washington, DC.

Capitol in the capital

Washington, DC, is the capital of the US and the home of its government. Senators and congressmen meet in the Capitol building to make laws.

Independence Day

The US became an independent country on July 4, 1776. The Fourth of July is a holiday called Independence Day. There are parties and big parades through the streets.

The city of New Orleans is the home of jazz.

Musical roots

Modern rock and pop music grew from jazz and blues, which were invented by African Americans about 100 years ago.

Independence Day parade

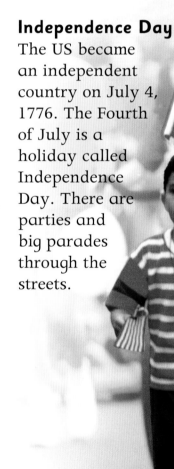

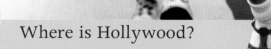

Where is Hollywood?

American food

The US has food as varied as its people.

Hamburgers are not made from ham, but from ground beef.

Clam chowder is seafood soup from New England.

Tex-Mex is a mixture of flavors from Texas and Mexico.

Gumbo is a spicy soup from Louisiana, made with meat and seafood.

American Indians

American Indians have lived in the US for thousands of years. Today, about one in 100 Americans is American Indian.

These girls are wearing the traditional clothes of Navajo Indians. The Navajo live in Arizona and New Mexico.

Football

Football

The top spectator sport in the US is football. More than 40 million people a year go to watch games, often in big stadiums.

Rodeo rider on a bull

The Oscar award is given for excellence in filmmaking.

© A.M.P.A.S.®

Rodeo rider

People visit rodeos to watch cowboys show off their riding skills. The cowboy tries to stay on a bucking horse or bull as long as he can.

Film industry

American movies are watched all over the world. Hollywood is the home of the film industry.

In the city of Los Angeles, California.

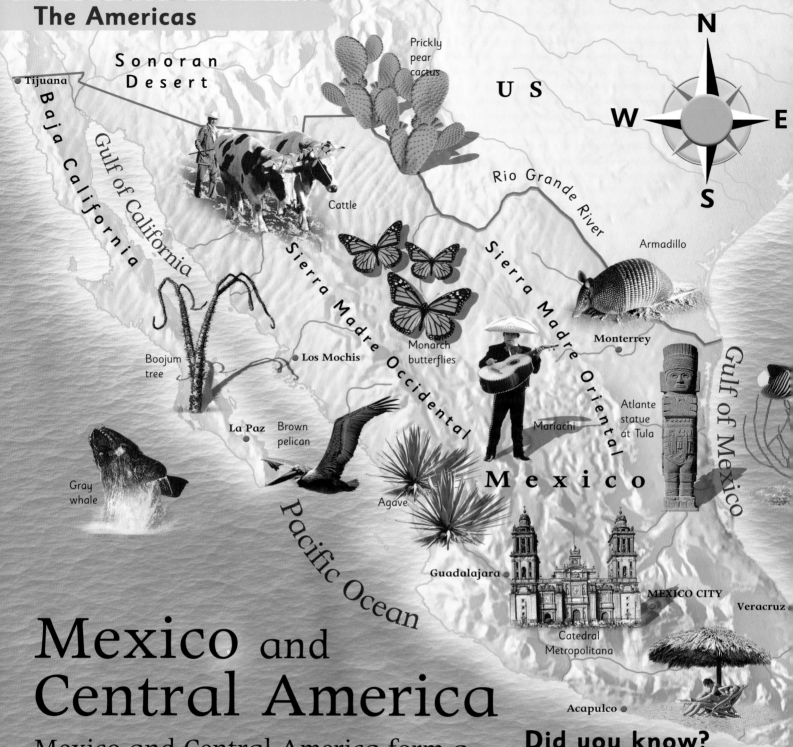

Sonoran Desert

Prickly pear cactus

Tijuana

U S

Baja California

Gulf of California

Cattle

Rio Grande River

Sierra Madre Occidental

Sierra Madre Oriental

Armadillo

Monarch butterflies

Monterrey

Boojum tree

Los Mochis

Gulf of Mexico

Gray whale

La Paz

Brown pelican

Mariachi

Atlante statue at Tula

M e x i c o

Agave

Pacific Ocean

Guadalajara

MEXICO CITY

Veracruz

Catedral Metropolitana

Acapulco

Mexico and Central America

Mexico and Central America form a natural bridge linking the US to South America. Northern Mexico is dry and dusty. As you travel south, the weather gets rainier and the land becomes greener, with lush rainforests covering mountains and volcanoes.

Did you know?

Coffee beans and bananas are Costa Rica's most important crops.

Chocolate was first made in Mexico, from the seeds of the cacao tree.

Sugar cane from Central America and the Caribbean is used to make sugar.

How do spider monkeys use their tails?

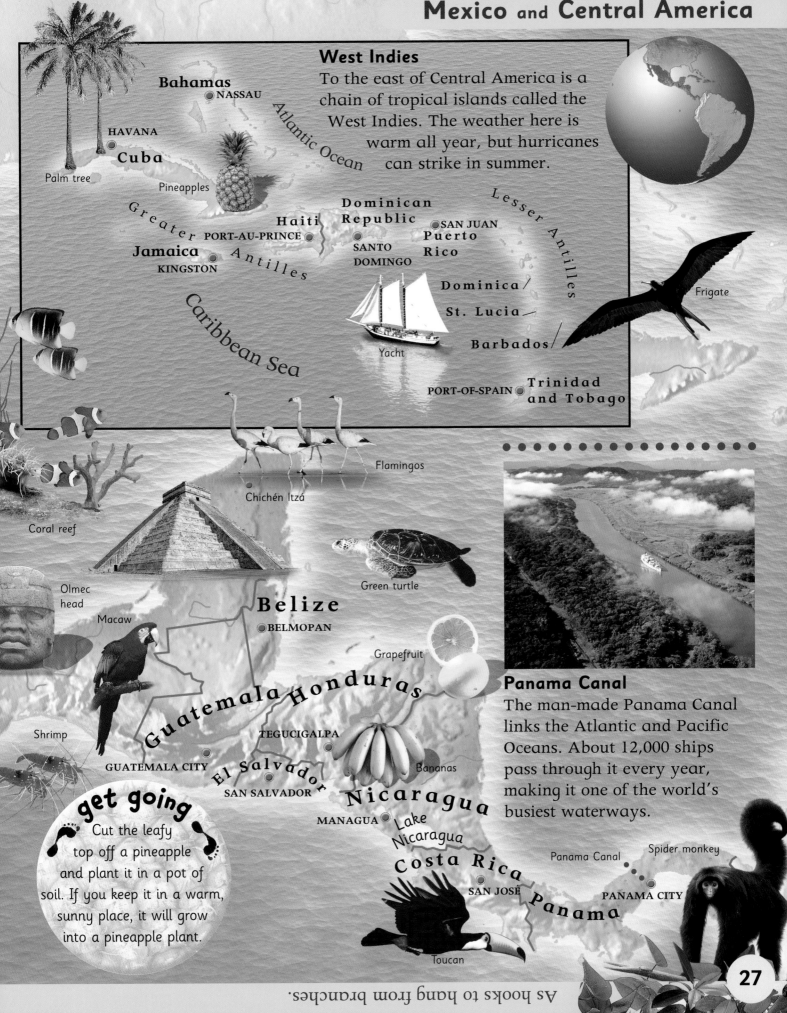

West Indies

To the east of Central America is a chain of tropical islands called the West Indies. The weather here is warm all year, but hurricanes can strike in summer.

Bahamas

NASSAU

HAVANA

Cuba

Palm tree

Pineapples

Atlantic Ocean

Greater Antilles

Haiti

PORT-AU-PRINCE

Jamaica

KINGSTON

Dominican Republic

SANTO DOMINGO

SAN JUAN

Puerto Rico

Lesser Antilles

Dominica

St. Lucia

Barbados

Frigate

Caribbean Sea

Yacht

PORT-OF-SPAIN

Trinidad and Tobago

Flamingos

Chichén Itzá

Coral reef

Olmec head

Green turtle

Macaw

Belize

BELMOPAN

Grapefruit

Panama Canal

The man-made Panama Canal links the Atlantic and Pacific Oceans. About 12,000 ships pass through it every year, making it one of the world's busiest waterways.

Shrimp

Guatemala

Honduras

TEGUCIGALPA

GUATEMALA CITY

El Salvador

SAN SALVADOR

Bananas

Nicaragua

MANAGUA

Lake Nicaragua

Panama Canal

Spider monkey

Costa Rica

SAN JOSÉ

Panama

PANAMA CITY

get going

Cut the leafy top off a pineapple and plant it in a pot of soil. If you keep it in a warm, sunny place, it will grow into a pineapple plant.

As hooks to hang from branches.

Toucan

27

Mexico and Central America

Mexico and Central America are a melting pot of bustling cities, ancient ruins, and steamy jungles. Most of the people speak Spanish.

Aztecs and Mayas

Hundreds of years ago, the Aztec and Maya peoples built fabulous cities in the jungles and mountains. Their crumbling ruins survive to this day.

This man is dressed as an Aztec warrior. The Aztecs used to sacrifice their enemies and rip their hearts out.

Around 1,000 years ago, this pyramid was the center of a huge Mayan city called Chichén Itzá.

What is the name for a Mexican flatbread made from corn and flour?

Agriculture

Central America is warm and wet—perfect weather for tropical crops like bananas, corn, avocados, and peppers. Farmers sell their crops in the busy local markets.

Mexico City

Mexico's capital was built on the ruins of an ancient Aztec city. It is now one of the world's biggest cities, with 20 million people.

Tacos and tortillas

Mexicans like spicy food flavored with chili peppers. These are tacos—fried corn tortillas filled with meat and vegetables.

Caribbean paradise

The sunny islands of the Caribbean attract tourists by the million. They come to laze on beautiful, sandy beaches, swim in the warm sea, and snorkel over coral reefs.

get going

Get a slice of bread and roll it out flat using a rolling pin. Now add your favorite filling and roll the bread around it. You've just made a Mexican enchilada!

A tortilla (pronounced "tor-TEE-ya").

South America

A vast chain of mountains runs the length of this continent. On its western side is the world's driest desert. On the east is the biggest rainforest.

Equator walkabout

The equator is an imaginary line around Earth's middle. It would take you a month to walk across just the South American part of it!

Bananas

Brazil nuts

Belém

Capybara

Brazil

CAYENNE

PARAMARIBO

French Guiana

Suriname

GEORGETOWN

Guyana

Angel Falls

Orinoco

CARACAS

Venezuela

Cartagena

Agrias butterfly

BOGOTÁ

Colombia

QUITO

Ecuador

Equator

Amazon Rainforest

Manaus

Amazon River

Jaguar

Parakeet

Condor

Peru

LIMA

Machu Picchu

Andes Mountains

Lake Titicaca

Arequipa

Bolivia

LA PAZ

Arica

Pacific Ocean

30

What is the highest mountain in the Andes?

• Salvador

Oil rig

Soccer

• Brasília Catheural
◉ **BRASÍLIA**

São Paulo • • Rio de Janeiro

Sugar Loaf Mountain

Atlantic Ocean

Green turtle

Gaucho

Paraguay

• ASUNCIÓN

Bolivian Indian

Llama

Argentina

Uruguay

Pampas grass

◉ MONTEVIDEO

BUENOS AIRES

Pampas

Bahía Blanca

Chile

Atacama Desert

Andes Mountains

Aconcagua

Valparaíso • • SANTIAGO

Mackerel

Sheep farming

Patagonia

Magellan penguins

Cape Horn

Cape Horn

The southern tip of South America is called Cape Horn. The seas around it are so stormy that hundreds of ships have been shipwrecked there.

Can you find...

The world's highest capital?
La Paz, Bolivia, is 11,916 ft (3,632 m) above sea level.

The world's highest waterfall?
Angel Falls in Venezuela measures 3,212 ft (979 m) from top to bottom.

The world's driest town?
Arica in Chile's Atacama Desert has an annual rainfall of zero!

Aconcagua, which is 22,834 ft (6,960 m) high.

South America

One-third of South America is covered by a huge jungle called the Amazon rainforest. To the east and south of the rainforest are rich grasslands, enormous cattle ranches, and South America's biggest cities.

Scarlet macaw

Forest life

Native people have lived in the Amazon jungle for thousands of years. They survive by hunting and gathering wild food, without harming the forest.

Yanomami village in the Amazon rainforest.

Deadly animals

The Amazon rainforest is home to all sorts of dangerous creatures.

Gauchos

Argentinian gauchos are like American cowboys. They work on vast ranches in the pampas grasslands of Argentina, where they look after cattle and horses.

Forest people use **poison-dart frogs** to make deadly poison for arrows.

The **jaguar** is a very secretive cat. It is a good swimmer and climber.

Piranhas are vicious fish with very sharp teeth. They hunt in packs.

The **boa constrictor** kills animals by squeezing them to death.

Dugout canoe on the Amazon

What language do most Brazilians speak?

Highest waterfall

Angel Falls in Venezuela is the world's highest waterfall. The water tumbles off a flat-topped mountain and plunges 3,215 ft (980 m) to the ground. That's three times the height of New York's Empire State Building.

Granadillas grow on jungle vines.

Forest fruits

The granadilla (a kind of passionfruit) is one of many exotic fruits that grow in tropical parts of South America.

Rio de Janeiro

A statue of Christ towers over Rio de Janeiro, Brazil's second-largest city. In the bay is the dome-shaped Sugar Loaf Mountain.

Carnival

Every year, Rio de Janeiro holds a spectacular carnival that lasts four days. People dress up in brilliant costumes and dance through the streets, blowing whistles and singing.

Portuguese.

Life in the Andes

The Andes stretch all the way down South America, forming the world's longest mountain range. The people and animals that live in the Andes are used to the cold, thin air.

Condor
The Andean condor is a huge bird of prey. In flight, its wings measure 10 ft (3 m) from tip to tip.

Machu Picchu
High in the Andes in Peru are the ruins of an ancient city called Machu Picchu. The city was built about 500 years ago by people called Incas.

Llamas
A llama is like a tall sheep. People in the Andes keep llamas for their warm wool, for their milk and meat, and for carrying cargo.

What is the most southerly city in the world?

Atacama Desert

The Atacama is the largest desert in South America. It is officially the driest place on Earth because it hardly ever rains here.

Valparaíso

Sandwiched between the mountains and the coast is Valparaíso, one of Chile's biggest cities. It is Chile's main port.

get going

Make some panpipes. Stick together ten straws with tape. Cut the bottoms of the straws at an angle. Blow across the straws to play the pipes.

Mountain people

Many people who live in the Andes are South American Indians. Their families have lived in the Andes for hundreds of years.

Panpipes

The panpipes are a traditional Andean musical instrument. They are made from hollow reeds or bamboo.

People from the Andean city of Cuzco, Peru, wear very colorful clothes.

Sailing on top of the world

At 12,450 ft (3,800 m) high, Lake Titicaca is the highest lake in the world that ships can sail on. Local people fish the lake in boats made from reeds.

Punta Arenas, Chile.

Africa

Africa is a vast, sun-baked continent, famous for its amazing wildlife. In the north and south are hot deserts. Between the deserts are swampy rainforests and grasslands full of wild animals.

N · E · W · S

Asia

Mediterranean Sea

Red Sea

Suez Canal

Nile River

Gulf of Sirte

CAIRO

Aswan

Pyramids

Egypt

Libya

TRIPOLI
Al 'Aziziyah

Bedouin weaver

TUNIS

Tunisia

ALGIERS

Algeria

Erg Tifernine

Ahaggar Mountains

Sahara Desert

Tuareg nomads

Ostriches

Ait Benhaddou mud fortress, Morocco

Atlas Mountains

RABAT

Morocco

Western Sahara

LAAYOUNE

Atlantic Ocean

Mauritania

NOUAKCHOTT

Peanuts

Mali

BAMAKO

Bambara village

Niger River

Niger

Sahel

NIAMEY

Lake Chad

Chad

Lake Chad

NDJAMENA

Nubian Desert

Nile felucca boat

KHARTOUM

Sudan

Southern Sudan

Cheetah

Hippopotamus

Lion

Central African Rep.

BANGU

Cameroon

ABUJA

Nigeria

Benin

Togo

Ghana

Burkina Faso

Côte d'Ivoire

Cocoa bean

Guinea

Sierra Leone

Liberia

Guinea-Bissau

Gambia

Senegal

DAKAR

Eritrea

ASMARA

Djibouti

Horn of Africa

ADDIS ABABA

East African Rift

Ethiopia

How long is Africa from north to south?

MOGADISHU

Som

Dhow sailing boat

Lemur

ANTANANARIVO

Chameleon

Madagascar

Madagascar
The island of Madagascar is home to tree-dwelling animals called lemurs. They have faces like cats but bodies like monkeys.

Kenya
Uganda
NAIROBI
Mount Kilimanjaro
KAMPALA
Lake Victoria
DODOMA
Serengeti
Tanzania
Rwanda
Burundi
Tea

Mozambique Channel

Malawi
East African Rift
Masai herder
Elephant

Dem. Rep. of Congo
Rwanda
Burundi
KINSHASA
Diamond mine
Lowland gorilla

Zambia
LUSAKA
Zambezi River

Zimbabwe
Mozambique

MAPUTO
Swaziland
PRETORIA

Lesotho
Ndeble house

Angola
Zebra

Congo River
Gabon
bananas
Equatorial Guinea

Namibia
WINDHOEK
Giraffe
Hornbill
Namib Desert
Victoria Falls
Botswana
Kalahari Desert
Tin and copper mining
Springbok
Cape Town
South Africa
Cape of Good Hope

LUANDA
Oil rig

Atlantic Ocean

Can you find...

The highest point in Africa?
Mount Kilimanjaro in Tanzania is 19,341 ft (5,895 m) tall.

One of the world's highest sand dunes? Erg Tifernine in the Sahara is 1,300 ft (400 m) tall.

The hottest place on Earth?
Al 'Aziziyah, in Libya, has had temperatures of 136.4°F (58°C).

The Suez Canal
This canal is a man-made waterway that runs from the Red Sea to the Mediterranean. It provides a shortcut for ships traveling from Europe to Asia.

Savanna wildlife
Much of Africa is covered by a type of grassland called savanna. Huge herds of grazing animals live on the savanna, along with lions, hyenas, and cheetahs.

Life in Africa

There are about 50 countries in Africa, but hundreds of different peoples and more than 1,000 languages. Most African people are farmers who live in the country. In recent times, many people have moved into cities.

Villagers in Ghana carrying water

Health and disease

Poor health is a problem in some parts of Africa. Many Africans have to walk for hours every day to get clean water. Diseases such as malaria are common.

Mosquitoes spread malaria when they bite people.

Masai people often wear lots of red to scare off lions.

Masai necklaces

The Masai people of east Africa lead a traditional way of life, herding their cows across the land. Masai women wear colorful beaded necklaces to show off how rich they are.

What is the world's largest continent?

Living in the city

One out of every five Africans lives in bustling cities, such as Cape Town. People move to the cities to find work and a better life.

Drummers from Ghana

African music

Africa people love music and dancing. These musicians come from Ghana in west Africa. Their drums are made from animal skins pulled tight by strings.

Safaris save animals

Tourists come to Africa's savanna (grassland) to see the wildlife. The money the tourists spend helps to save rare animals, such as rhinos.

Rainforest life

In the rainforests of central Africa, some people get their food from the wild. They travel through the forest, hunting animals and gathering fruit.

Animals roam the savanna in huge herds.

Asia. Africa is the second-largest.

African deserts

The biggest desert in the world, the Sahara, stretches right across northern Africa. Two more deserts, the Namib and the Kalahari, are located in southern Africa.

Trading in the desert

The Tuareg people are traders who live in the Sahara Desert. The men cover their faces with long blue scarves.

Water in the desert

An oasis is a spot in a desert where water comes up from underground, allowing plants to grow and people or animals to drink.

The Tuareg travel by camel, motorbike, and truck.

Camels can carry heavy loads.

What does a camel store in its hump?

Saharan wildlife

The Sahara is baking hot by day and freezing cold at night. Even so, lots of animals live there.

The **fennec fox** has huge ears that let heat escape from its body.

Horned vipers lie hidden in sand, looking for animals to eat.

The **jerboa** gets all the water it needs from the seeds it eats.

Desert locusts form huge swarms that can destroy crops.

A **scorpion** has a stinger at the end of its tail for killing the animals it eats.

Desert nomads

Desert nomads spend their lives on the move. They travel from oasis to oasis by camel and live in tents.

The San

The San are people from the Kalahari Desert. Today many San live in villages and towns, but some still lead a traditional way of life, moving around the desert hunting for food.

The San use hollow ostrich eggs as flasks to carry water in the desert.

get going

Make a nomad's tent. Throw a large sheet over a table so that it hangs down to the floor. Cover the floor under the table with colorful rugs and comfy cushions.

San hunters with poisoned arrows

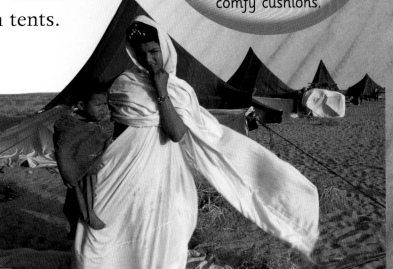

Dogon dancers

The Dogon people live in Mali on the edge of the Sahara Desert. These Dogon are imitating long-legged birds in a traditional stilt dance.

Fat.

The Nile River

Life in northeast Africa would be impossible without the Nile, the world's longest river. It flows across the Sahara Desert, providing vital water and a highway for boats.

Lake Victoria is the main source of the Nile.

The route of the Nile
The Nile begins in Uganda and flows 4,200 miles (6,700 km) north, passing through Sudan and Egypt.

Aswan dams
At Aswan in Egypt, two huge dams have been built to store water and to generate electricity.

Sailing the Nile

In Egypt, people sail up and down the Nile on wooden boats called feluccas. It hardly ever rains in Egypt, so the crew sleeps on the open deck at night.

Abu Simbel
The Abu Simbel temples were built by the ancient Egyptians. Engineers moved them to save them from being drowned when the Aswan High Dam was built.

Who was buried in Egypt's biggest pyramid?

City on the Nile

Cairo is the capital of Egypt and the biggest city in Africa. Around 10 million people live in Cairo, many of them in crowded slums.

Nile Delta from space

Nile Delta

The Nile dumps lots of silt at its mouth, forming a muddy area called a delta. Crops grow especially well here.

Nile crops

These crops grow on the banks of the Nile.

Wheat is grown for making flour, which is used in bread-making.

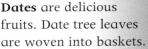

Dates are delicious fruits. Date tree leaves are woven into baskets.

Fibers from **cotton seeds** are used to make yarn and fabrics.

The Pyramids

Huge pyramids stand in the desert near Cairo. The pyramids were built thousands of years ago as tombs for ancient kings called pharaohs.

The Sphinx has a lion's body and a man's head.

Egyptian farmers use donkeys to pull carts.

Farming on the Nile

Farmers take water from the Nile to irrigate their fields. There is a narrow strip of farmland on each bank of the river. The Sahara Desert lies beyond the fields.

Pharaoh Khufu (Cheops).

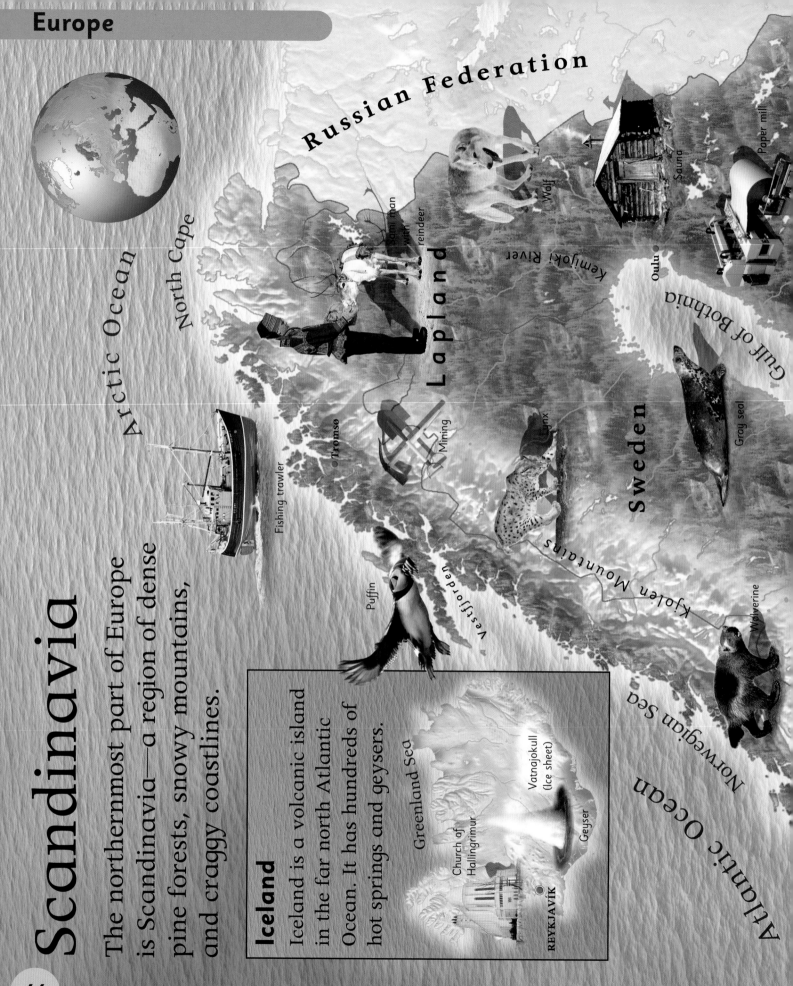

Scandinavia

The northernmost part of Europe is Scandinavia—a region of dense pine forests, snowy mountains, and craggy coastlines.

Iceland

Iceland is a volcanic island in the far north Atlantic Ocean. It has hundreds of hot springs and geysers.

Greenland Sea

Church of Hallingrimur

Vatnajokull (Ice sheet)

Geyser

REYKJAVIK

Russian Federation

Arctic Ocean

North Cape

Sami man with reindeer

Wolf

Sauna

Paper mill

Kemijoki River

Oulu

Lapland

Gulf of Bothnia

Fishing trawler

Tromsø

Mining

Lynx

Sweden

Gray seal

Puffin

Vestfjorden

Kjølen Mountains

Wolverine

Norwegian Sea

Atlantic Ocean

Which Scandinavian warriors raided Europe in AD 800–1050?

Finland

Rainbow trout

Cathedral, Helsinki

HELSINKI

Gulf of Finland

Åland Islands

STOCKHOLM

The Øresund Bridge

The Øresund Bridge links Copenhagen, Denmark, to Malmö, Sweden. There are three parts to the bridge—an underground tunnel, an artificial island, and a bridge over the sea. Together, they are 10 miles (16 km) long.

Gotland

Rune stone

City Hall, Stockholm

Golden eagle

Lake Vättern

Öland

Baltic Sea

Swedish glass

N
W — E
S

Bornholm

Cross-country skiing

Lake Vänern

Gothenburg

COPENHAGEN

Malmö

Stave church

Norway

Mount Galdhøppigen 8,100 ft (2,469 m)

OSLO

Oslo Fjord

Sculptures in Vigeland Park, Oslo

Little Mermaid statue, Copenhagen

Nord Fjord

Sogne Fjord

Bergen

Hardanger Fjord

Boknn Fjord

Stavanger

Dairy farming

Denmark

Pig farming

Lego

Faeroe Islands

These islands are part of Denmark. They lie halfway between Iceland and Scotland.

North Sea

Herring

Scandinavia

Ski-jumper, Norway

Scandinavians enjoy a spectacular landscape and a high standard of living. But they also have to cope with long, dark, icy winters.

Pine forests cover much of Scandinavia.

Winter sports
Winter sports are very popular in Scandinavia. Many top ski-jumpers come from this region.

All the houses in Legoland are built from Lego.

Legoland
The Legoland theme park in Denmark is built from 50 million Lego™ bricks. Lego was invented in Denmark in 1949.

Viking ships
The Vikings lived in Scandinavia 1,000 years ago. They raided other countries in longships like this one.

Logging industry
In Scandinavia, millions of trees are grown for their wood. The lumber is made into houses, furniture, and paper.

What is a Finnish steam room called?

Wildlife

The animals that live in Scandinavia are well adapted to the cold.

Arctic foxes have thick white fur for warmth and camouflage in the snow.

The **lynx** is a type of cat from the forests of Norway and Sweden.

Puffins are small seabirds. They swim underwater to catch fish.

Elks are large deer. Their huge antlers can be 6.5 ft (2 m) wide.

Naturally hot
Iceland has many volcanoes, geysers, and hot springs. The water in this lake is heated by hot rocks deep underground.

Norwegian fjords

Hundreds of narrow valleys cut into the coast of Norway. They are called fjords. Ships can shelter here from bad weather.

Lapland

Northern Scandinavia is called Lapland. The people who live there are Sami (or Lapps). Some Sami herd reindeer for their fur, meat, and milk.

A sauna.

UK and Ireland

The United Kingdom is made up of England, Scotland, Wales, and Northern Ireland. Ireland is a separate country. Most of the people in the UK and Ireland speak English as their main language.

The Royal Family

England and Scotland had separate royal families until 1603, when they joined together to form the United Kingdom. Queen Elizabeth II is the current head of state.

Shetland Islands

Orkney Islands

Thurso

Red deer

Loch Ness Monster

Aberdeen

Grampian Mountains

North Sea

Ben Nevis
4,406 ft (1,343 m)

Scotland

Forth River

Bagpiper

Edinburgh

Angel of the North

Newcastle upon Tyne

Outer Hebrides

Skye

Highland cow

Mull

Glasgow

Giant's Causeway

Edinburgh Castle

Northern Ireland

Belfast

What is the name of the Queen's official residence in London?

North Sea
oil rig

Yacht

Norfolk
Broads

Cambridge

Dover

Eurotunnel
to France

Middlesbrough

Kingston
upon Hull

Big Ben

LONDON

Pennines

England

Birmingham

Oxford

Thames River

Brighton

Royal Pavilion

English Channel

France

Lake
District

Blackpool
Tower

Manchester

Football

Crufts
dog show

Severn River

Stonehenge

Isle of Wight

Liverpool

Snowdonia

Cambrian
Mountains

Wales

Cardiff

Portland
Bill
lighthouse

Douglas

Isle of Man

Irish Sea

Sheep

Exmoor

Dartmoor

Exeter

The Eden Project

These giant greenhouses are
home to lots of plants from
different areas of the world.
People can visit here to learn
how important nature is to the
future of the planet.

Guinness

DUBLIN

Surfing

Eden Project

Galway
Cathedral

Ireland

Blarney
Castle

Galway

Cork

Land's
End

Isles of Scilly

N
E
S
W

Jaunting car

Buckingham Palace.

49

UK and Ireland

The islands that make up the UK and Ireland are called the British Isles. The British Isles are famous for their history, traditions, and for their green—though rainy—countryside.

The London Eye

London is the capital of the UK and the site of the London Eye—a gigantic ferris wheel that gives tourists a stunning view over the city.

Passengers ride the Eye in glass capsules.

Fish and chips

British food has been influenced by many cultures, but fish and "chips" (French fries) is a popular traditional dish.

Stately home

Windsor Castle near London is one of the Queen's homes. It is the largest occupied castle in the world and has around 1,000 rooms. Certain parts of the castle are open to tourists.

Grenadier guards wear a tall hat made from the fur of Canadian black bears.

The Queen's private army of guards are called beefeaters.

Which Welsh village has the longest place name in Europe?

At the pub

Nearly every town and village in the UK and Ireland boasts at least one pub, where people go to relax and meet their friends. Irish pubs serve a famous type of beer called Guinness, which is dark brown and frothy.

A pint of Guinness

British sports

Sports invented by the British are now played all over the world.

Cricket is played in summer. Some matches last for five days.

Soccer is the world's most popular sport, watched by billions.

Rugby is played with an oval ball that the players pick up and run with.

Scottish lakes are called lochs.

Rocky coast

Rugged cliffs and strange rock formations dot the north coast of Northern Ireland. The wobbly Carrick-a-rede Rope Bridge leads to a tiny island.

Highland cow

Soccer and rugby

Soccer and rugby matches attract huge crowds of fans in the UK. English and Scottish people are great soccer fans. Welsh people also like rugby.

Scottish highlands

Northern Scotland has some of the UK's quietest countryside, with miles of rolling mountains and glassy lakes. There are few people here, apart from farmers and hikers.

The Low Countries

Belgium, the Netherlands, and Luxembourg are called the Low Countries because they are so flat. They are also sometimes called Benelux—the first letters of BElgium, NEtherlands and LUXembourg.

Netherlands

Germany

Avocet

Cattle

Cyclist

Horses

Ice skating

West Frisian Islands

Waddenzee

IJsselmeer

Flevoland

Windmills

Rhine River

Arnhem

Clogs

Eindhoven

Tern

Cheese porters

AMSTERDAM

Tulips

Rotterdam

Barge

Antwerp Cathedral

North Sea

The Hague

Cubic Houses

Fishing

Herring

Dams to stop floods from sea

Bruges Town Hall

Bruges

Ostend

N E S W

What is another name for the Netherlands?

Did you know..?

Brussels is the capital of Europe. It is the center of the European Union and home of the European Parliament.

900 windmills along the Netherlands' coast help to keep the land drained.

Wooden clogs were invented by Dutch workers 600 years ago.

Belgium

The Atomium

BRUSSELS ○

Chocolates

Lace-making

France

Crystal

Liège

Charleroi

Beer

Meuse River

Deer

Ardennes

Ardennes Forest

Wild boar

Vianden castle

Luxembourg

LUXEMBOURG ○

Amsterdam

The tall houses lining the canals of Amsterdam were built by rich spice merchants hundreds of years ago. Each one is unique, and many are crooked because they are built on marshy land.

Holland.

The Low Countries

Large parts of the Low Countries used to be underwater, but people learned how to turn the shallow sea into farmland. The area is now famous for growing flowers.

Amsterdam

People sometimes call Amsterdam "the Venice of the north" because the city is riddled with canals and full of beautiful old houses. Cycling is popular because there are few cars in the center of town and no hills.

The Dutch make 3 million pairs of clogs (wooden shoes) each year. Farmers used to wear shoes like this for working in marshy fields.

get going

Make a windmill. Cut a cross from paper 4 in (10 cm) across. Twist each arm slightly the same way. Pin the center to a pencil and blow on the back to make it spin.

Cheese market

On Fridays, Dutch cheese-makers hold a traditional market in the town of Alkmaar to sell huge wheels of cheese. The most popular cheeses are Edam, which is covered with red wax, and Gouda.

How much of the Netherlands used to be under the sea?

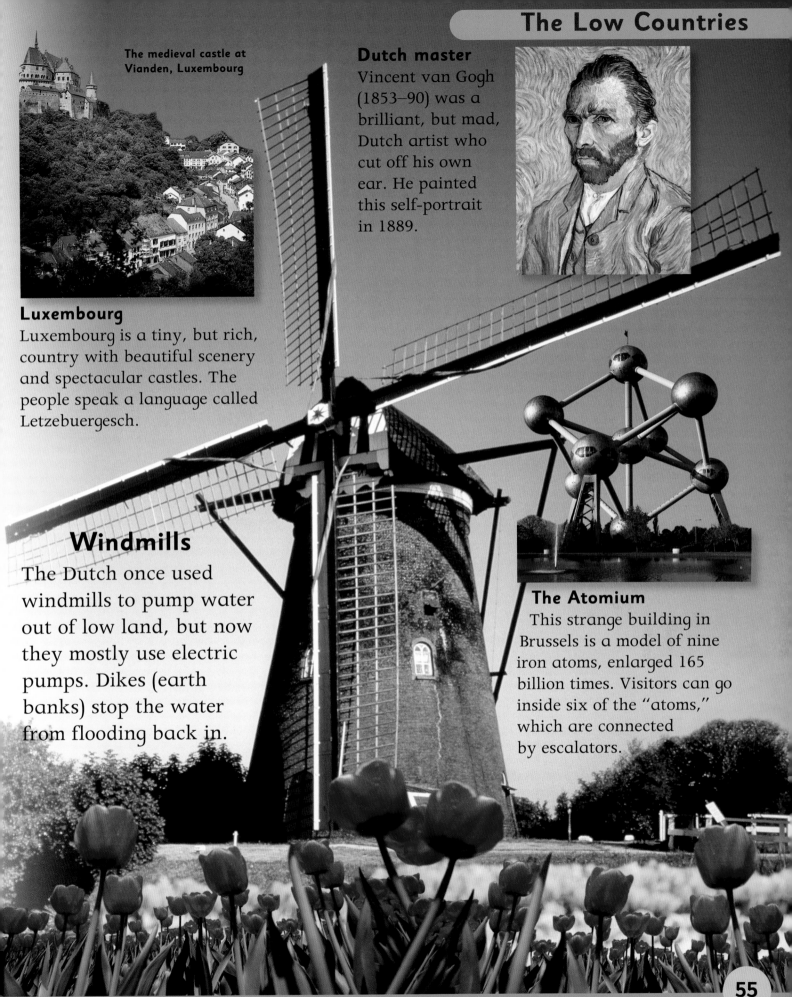

The medieval castle at Vianden, Luxembourg

Dutch master
Vincent van Gogh (1853–90) was a brilliant, but mad, Dutch artist who cut off his own ear. He painted this self-portrait in 1889.

Luxembourg
Luxembourg is a tiny, but rich, country with beautiful scenery and spectacular castles. The people speak a language called Letzebuergesch.

Windmills
The Dutch once used windmills to pump water out of low land, but now they mostly use electric pumps. Dikes (earth banks) stop the water from flooding back in.

The Atomium
This strange building in Brussels is a model of nine iron atoms, enlarged 165 billion times. Visitors can go inside six of the "atoms," which are connected by escalators.

About one-third.

France

France is the biggest country in western Europe. Its capital is the city of Paris, site of the Eiffel Tower. France is famous for its scenic countryside, which is dotted with sleepy villages and fairy-tale castles called chateaus.

Mont-Saint-Michel

A towering abbey sits on the island of Mont-Saint-Michel off the north coast of France. At low tide, people can walk across the sand to get to the island.

English Channel

Breton woman

Mont-Saint-Michel

Bayeux Tapestry

Rennes

Le Mans race track

Le Mans

Standing Stones (Carnac)

Mackerel

Beef cattle

Brandy

Atlantic Ocean

Bordeaux

Wine

Biarritz

Bay of Biscay

Airplane manufacturing

Cave Paintings at Lascaux

Toulous

Pyrenees Mountains

Where in France would you find pink flamingos and wild horses?

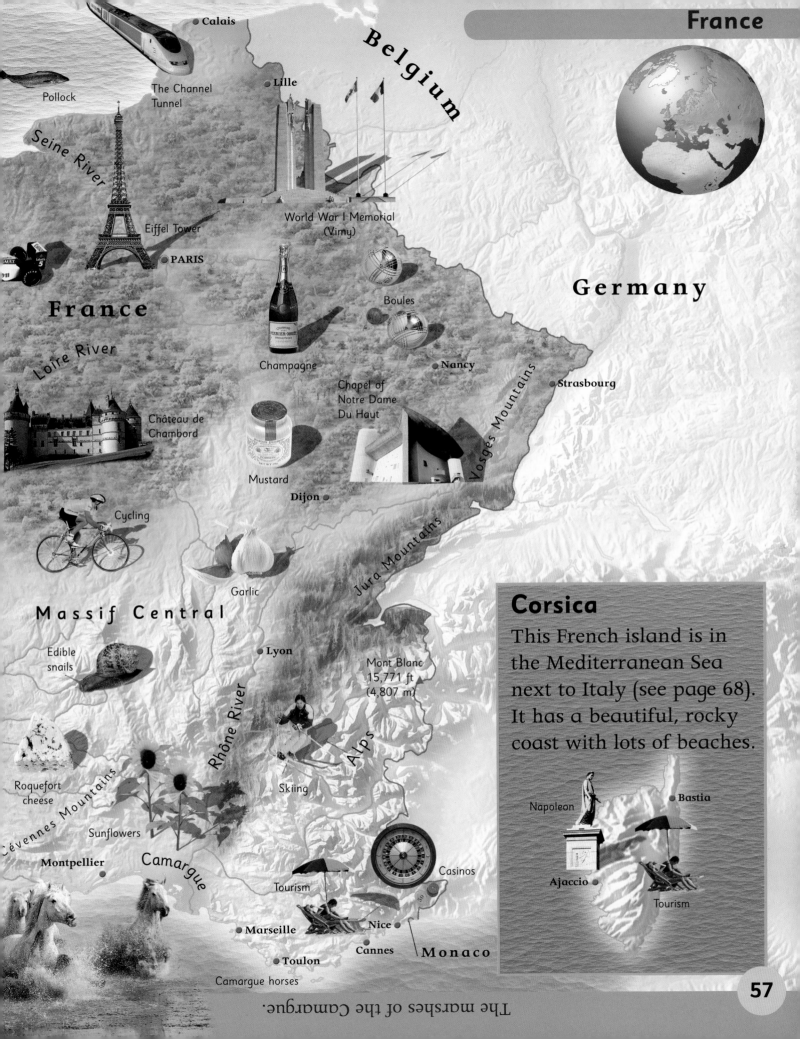

Calais

Pollock

The Channel Tunnel

Lille

Belgium

World War I Memorial (Vimy)

Seine River

Eiffel Tower

PARIS

France

Germany

Loire River

Champagne

Boules

Nancy

Strasbourg

Château de Chambord

Mustard

Chapel of Notre Dame Du Haut

Vosges Mountains

Dijon

Cycling

Jura Mountains

Garlic

Massif Central

Lyon

Mont Blanc 15,771 ft (4,807 m)

Edible snails

Rhône River

Roquefort cheese

Cévennes Mountains

Skiing

Alps

Sunflowers

Montpellier

Camargue

Tourism

Casinos

Marseille

Nice

Cannes

Monaco

Toulon

Camargue horses

Corsica

This French island is in the Mediterranean Sea next to Italy (see page 68). It has a beautiful, rocky coast with lots of beaches.

Napoleon

Bastia

Ajaccio

Tourism

The marshes of the Camargue.

France

Perfumes, bread, edible snails, and champagne are a few of the things that France is famous for. Millions of tourists visit Paris each year to see its beautiful buildings, parks, and museums.

Café culture
French people love to sit in cafés and watch the world go by. This café is on a wide avenue called the Champs-Élysées.

A famous landmark

The Eiffel Tower is the most famous landmark in France. It is 984 ft (300 m) high and was built in 1889. Tourists can go up to the top platform.

Visitors can walk up to the lower floors.

get going
Fields of sunflowers are a common sight in France. Grow your own sunflower by planting a seed in a pot of soil in spring. Water it every week and it will be taller than you are by summer.

How many people visit the Eiffel Tower each year?

Food and wine

French restaurants serve some of the best food in the world. France is also famous for making wine.

Snails are a French delicacy. They are cooked in their shells with garlic.

Croissants are made from flaky pastry. People eat them for breakfast.

Champagne is sparkling white wine. It is made in an area called Champagne.

Luxury houses

A large French country house is called a chateau. This one is Château d'Azay-le-Rideau. It was built 500 years ago and is surrounded by a lake.

Fast trains

The French TGV is the fastest express train in the world. It speeds along its special track at 190 miles (300 km) per hour.

Cyclists on the Tour de France, a three-week race.

Cheese-making

France makes 400 kinds of cheese, many of which are eaten all over the world. This cheese-maker taps the cheese to see if it has any holes.

Cycle racing

The Tour de France is the world's greatest cycle race and lasts for thousands of miles. French people stop work or school to watch the cyclists as they ride through town.

About 200 cyclists enter the race.

Many French farmers grow grapes for making wine.

About 6 million.

Germany and the Alps

Northern Germany is low and flat, but the land gradually rises toward the south. Switzerland and Austria lie in the heart of the Alps—Europe's tallest and most spectacular mountains.

Berlin Wall

A long wall used to divide the city of Berlin into communist and western halves. In 1989 the people of Berlin tore the wall down and reunited the city.

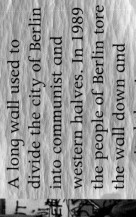

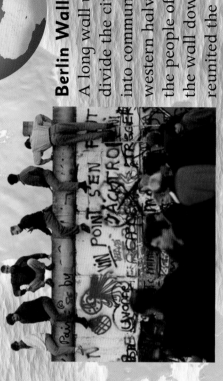

Poland

N
W S E

Oder River

Rügen

Stork

BERLIN

Brandenburg Gate

Chemical Industry

Zwinger Palace

Lake Müritz

Elbe River

Halle

Leipzig

Red deer

Fehmarn

Heidschnuke sheep

Volkswagen cars

Kiel Canal

Kiel

Elbe River

Hamburg

Hanover

Wheat

Bremen

Beef cattle.

Germany

North Sea

Container ship

Cologne Cathedral

Rhine River

Düsseldorf

Which composer was born in Salzburg, Austria, in 1756?

Czech Republic

France

Thuringian Forest

Bonn

Frankfurt skyline

Frankfurt

Mannheim

Heidelberg

Wine

Main River

Nuremberg

Mercedes

Stuttgart

Swabian Alps

Black Forest

Freiburg

Rhine River

Danube River

Ulm

Cheese

Neuschwanstein
Castle

Lake Constance

Zurich

Chocolate

BERN

Switzerland

Swiss Alps

Swiss
army knife

Rhône River

Matterhorn
14,692 ft
(4,478 m)

Geneva

Bohemian Forest

Oktoberfest

Munich

Lake
Chiemsee

Bavarian Alps

Zugspitze
9,718 ft
(2,962 m)

Marmot

VADUZ

Davos

Liechtenstein

Alpine
horn

Linz

Danube River

Mozart

Salzburg

Austrian Alps

Innsbruck

Austria

Mountain-
climbing

Graz

Snow-
boarding

Chamois
goat

Spanish
riding
school

VIENNA

Neusiedler Lake

Germany and the Alps

Germany, Austria, and Switzerland are rich industrial countries. They make and export many high-quality goods, including cars, watches, and chocolates.

Ice has carved the peak of the Matterhorn into a pyramid shape.

Pyramid peak

The Matterhorn in Switzerland is one of the tallest mountains in the Alps. Some people have fallen to their death trying to climb it.

German industry

Volkswagens are made in Europe's biggest car factory, near Hanover, Germany. Car-making is one of Germany's main industries.

Winter sports

Millions of people come to the Alps every winter to ski and snowboard. Hikers and mountaineers walk in the valleys and scale the peaks.

How did farmers used to communicate in the Alps?

Alpine wildlife

Many plants and animals survive high in the Alps.

Edelweiss is a small flower that grows in Alpine meadows.

The **Alpine marmot** sleeps through the winter in its burrow.

The **chamois** grows a thick, woolly coat to keep it warm.

Viennese pastries are said to be the best cakes in the world.

Neuschwanstein in Bavaria was the inspiration for Sleeping Beauty's castle in Disneyland.

German castles

Fabulous castles are scattered among the mountains of southern Germany. Neuschwanstein was built in 1869 by an eccentric king called Ludwig II.

Carnival time

Germans celebrate the end of winter with carnivals. In Cologne, people dress up in bright costumes and join the parades.

Viennese coffee houses

Vienna, Austria, is famous for its coffee houses, where people drink coffee and eat expensive bakery.

Alpine cows have bells so that farmers don't lose them on the mountainside.

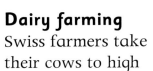

Germany's waterways

Germany's cities are linked by a large network of canals and rivers. This cargo barge is on the Neckar River in the city of Heidelberg.

Swiss people eat more chocolate than anyone else in the world.

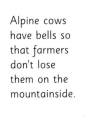

Dairy farming

Swiss farmers take their cows to high alpine meadows in summer. The cows' milk is used for making chocolates and cheese.

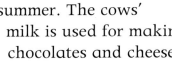

By yodeling (singing across mountain valleys).

Spain and Portugal

Spain and Portugal are in the sunny southwest corner of Europe. Together they make up a region called the Iberian Peninsula.

Azores

These Portuguese islands are in the Atlantic, about a third of the way to the US.

Dolphin

Ponta Delgada

Madeira

The Portuguese island of Madeira is famous for making a rich type of wine also called Madeira.

Grapes

Funchal

Canary Islands

These seven Spanish islands are off the west coast of Africa.

La Palma

Santa Cruz de Tenerife

Tenerife

Fuerteventura

Gran Canaria

Lanzarote

Banana plantations

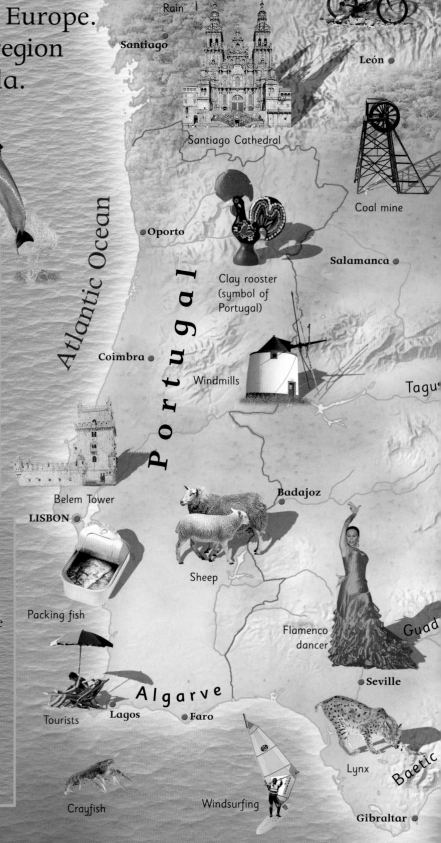

Mountain bike

Rain

Santiago

León

Santiago Cathedral

Coal mine

Oporto

Salamanca

Clay rooster (symbol of Portugal)

Atlantic Ocean

Coimbra

Portugal

Windmills

Tagu

Belem Tower

LISBON

Badajoz

Sheep

Flamenco dancer

Guad

Packing fish

Algarve

Seville

Tourists

Lagos

Faro

Lynx

Baetic

Crayfish

Windsurfing

Gibraltar

Which is the rainiest city in Spain?

Guggenheim
Museum

Bilbao

France

Andorra

**Basque
Country**

Mountain
goat

Pyrenees

ANDORRA
LA VELLA

Skiing

N

Wild boar

Iberian Mountains

Ebro River

Barcelona

W

E

Valladolid

Spain

Rioja wine

Sagrada Familia
Cathedral, Barcelona

S

Roman aqueduct

Sardines

Balearic Islands

Minorca

Mahón

MADRID

Majorca

iver

Palma

Mediterranean Sea

Bullfighting

Paella

Valencia

Royal Palace

Albacete

Ibiza

Ibiza

Oranges

Formentera

Alicante

Costa Blanca

Andalusian horse

quivir River

Andalusia

Guitar

Cartagena

Olives
and oil

Majorca

The Spanish
island of Majorca
is one of Europe's top
tourist destinations.
Its rugged coast has lots
of picturesque beaches.

Granada

ountains

Malaga

Costa del Sol

Jet-ski

Santiago.

Spain and Portugal

The streets of Spain and Portugal burst into life during their colorful festivals, or fiestas, but in the hot afternoons they can be sleepy and quiet.

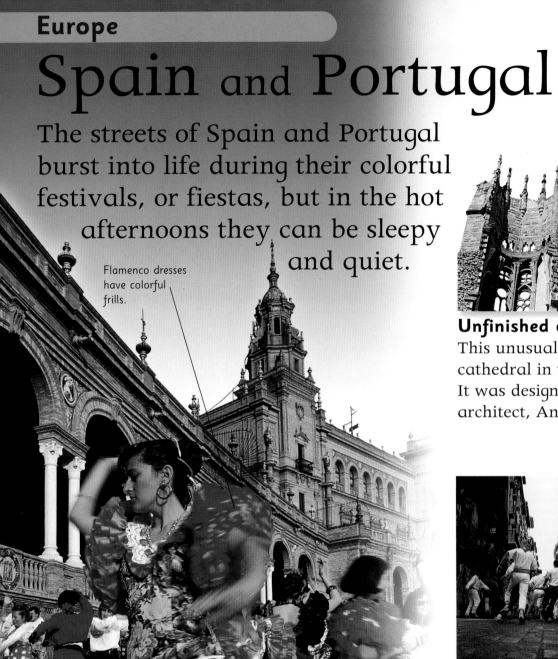

Flamenco dresses have colorful frills.

Unfinished cathedral
This unusual building is an unfinished cathedral in the Spanish city of Barcelona. It was designed by a famous Spanish architect, Antonio Gaudí (1852–1926).

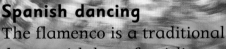

Bulls in the streets
Running from charging bulls is part of a festival held every July in the city of Pamplona. Hundreds of men run away from bulls that are let out in the streets.

Spanish dancing
The flamenco is a traditional dance with lots of twirling and stamping. It started in southern Spain about 500 years ago.

Paella
This traditional Spanish dish is made from yellow rice mixed with seafood, pieces of meat, tomatoes, and peppers.

Which city held the 1992 Olympic Games?

Algarve beaches

Portugal's southern coast is called the Algarve. This warm area has many sandy beaches and it is a popular spot with tourists from the rest of Europe.

The guitar is played by plucking the strings.

Classical guitar

Traditional Spanish music, including flamenco, is played on the classical guitar. The guitar was invented in Spain about 500 years ago.

Fishing industry

Bordered by the Atlantic Ocean and the Mediterranean Sea, Spain and Portugal have huge fishing industries. People who live on the coast eat lots of fish and seafood.

Traditional Portuguese fishing boats.

A2307M

A2220.M

Lobsters turn red when they are cooked. Living lobsters are blue-gray.

Italy

Italy is shaped like a boot, with the top in the Alps mountains and the toe dipping in the Mediterranean Sea. The Apennine mountains run like a bone down the leg.

Italian lakes

There are 23 lakes in the lake district in northern Italy. Lake Garda is the biggest, and a popular place to sail and windsurf.

Skier

Dolomites

A l p s

Mountain goat

Venice

Venetian gondola

Lake Garda

Ferrari

Po River

Tagliatelli carbonara

San Marino

Milan

Turin

Wine

Bologna

Leaning Tower of Pisa

Pisa

Florence

Florence Cathedral

Moped

Fishing boat

Tuna

How many islands make up Malta?

N E S W (compass)

Octopus

Crab

Wine

Taranto

Olives and olive oil

Sheep

Oranges

Pescara

Apennines

Italy

Vatican City

Pizza

Mount Vesuvius
Pompeii

Cast of a body at Pompeii

Naples

Amalfi

Squid

Almonds

Noto Cathedral

Messina

Syracuse

Mount Etna

Scuba diving

Can you find...

Europe's largest volcano?
Mount Etna in Sicily is also Europe's most active volcano.

The world's most tilted tower?
The Leaning Tower of Pisa is a campanile, or bell tower.

Where the first pizza was made? A baker in Naples invented the pizza in the 1800s.

ROME

The Colosseum (Rome)

Sardines

Sardinia

Tourism

Wild boar

Cagliari

Amalfi

Palermo

Sicily

Agrigento

Lemons

Temple of Castor and Pollux

Malta

VALLETTA

Mediterranean Sea

Italy

Italy has some of the world's most beautiful cities, and its museums contain priceless paintings and sculptures. Italy also has modern industries, such as car-making and electronics.

Vatican City

The Vatican City is the home of the Pope, the head of the Roman Catholic Church. It is the world's smallest state and has its own flag.

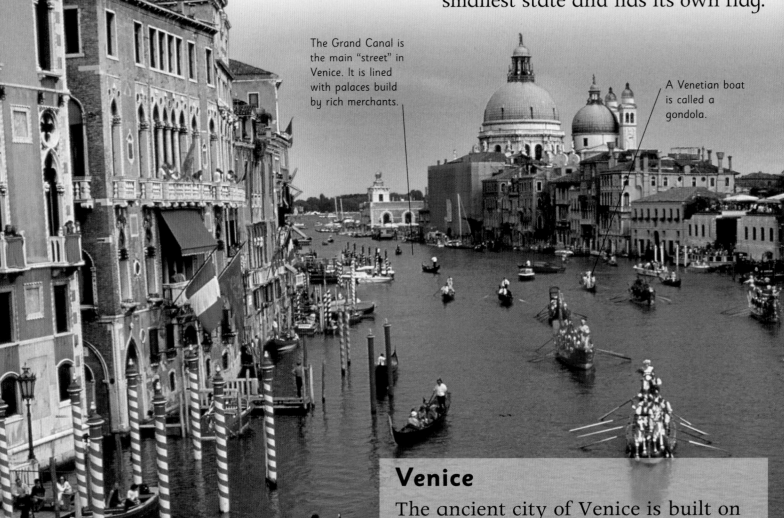

The Grand Canal is the main "street" in Venice. It is lined with palaces build by rich merchants.

A Venetian boat is called a gondola.

Venice

The ancient city of Venice is built on islands in the sea. Venice has canals and boats instead of streets and cars.

What were the people who lived in ancient Italy called?

Italian food

Italians enjoy eating with family and friends. Most meals include fresh vegetables and olive oil.

 Cappuccino is coffee with frothy milk. Italians drink many different kinds of coffee.

 Pasta is made in dozens of different shapes. This shape is called farfalle.

 Ice cream has been made in Italy for more than 500 years.

Painted chapel

The Sistine Chapel is in the Vatican. It was painted about 500 years ago by great Italian painters, including the famous artist and sculptor Michelangelo.

get going

Make a pizza from a piece of bread with some sliced tomatoes and cheese on top. Cook it under the broiler or in the oven until the cheese melts.

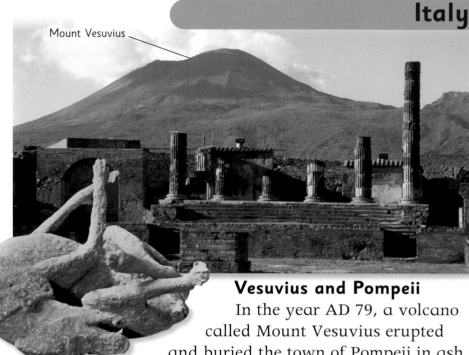

Mount Vesuvius

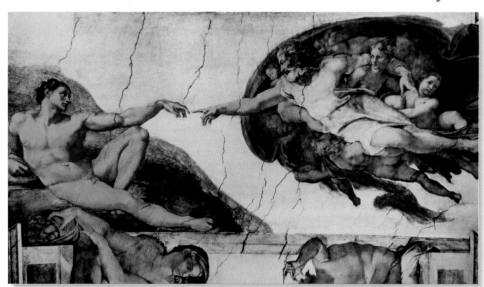

The cast of a dog killed at Pompeii

Vesuvius and Pompeii

In the year AD 79, a volcano called Mount Vesuvius erupted and buried the town of Pompeii in ash. The ruins of Pompeii and the remains of the volcano's victims can still be seen today.

It took Michelangelo four years to paint the ceiling of the Sistine Chapel, between 1508 and 1512.

Cars and scooters

Many famous makes of sports car come from Italy. This is a Ferrari. The streets of Italian towns and cities are full of buzzing scooters.

The Romans.

Central Eastern Europe

These countries were under communist rule until the 1990s. Today they are modern nations with thriving industries. Traditional farming continues in the rural areas.

Did you know?

The Polish town of Torun is well known for its **gingerbread**.

Budapest is split by the Danube. Buda is on one bank, Pest on the other.

The snow-white **Lipizzaner horse** is bred in Slovenia.

Baltic Sea

Canoeing

Mazury lakes

European bison

Chemical industry

Gingerbread

Torun

Market Square, Warsaw

Vistula River

Lublin

Sugar beet

Skiing

WARSAW

Wheat

Kielce

Cattle farms

Krakow

Gdansk

Potato farming

Lodz

Poland

Koszalin

Poznan

Pig farms

Oder River

Wroclaw

Windmills

Mining

Szczecin

Shipbuilding

Germany

Charles bridge

Karlovy Vary

PRAGUE

Hradec kralove

Elbe River

Plzen

What ingredient makes Hungarian goulash spicy?

Czech Republic

Pilsner lager

Brno

Skoda

Slovakia

High Tatra Mountains

Spissky Hrad castle

Painted Easter eggs

Wooden house

BRATISLAVA

Eger

Tokay wine

Nyiregyhaza

Debreen

Gyor

Parliament, Budapest

BUDAPEST

Szeged

Horses

Romania

Hungary

Danube River

Goulash

Pecs

Wine

Osijek

LJUBLJANA

ZAGREB

Slovenia

Croatia

Rijeka

Tourism

Dinaric Alps

Dalmatian

Split

Dubrovnik

Adriatic Sea

Austria

Lipizzaner mare and foal

High Tatra Mountains

This mountain range lies in Poland and Slovakia, and forms part of the Carpathian Mountains. The tallest peak is 8,710 ft (2,655 m) high.

N E S W

Paprika.

Central Eastern Europe

Winters bring deep snow to the plains and mountains of this part of Europe. Summers bring tourists to visit some of Europe's best preserved cities.

Vltava River, Prague

Old and modern

The capital of the Czech Republic is the historic city of Prague. It is full of ancient buildings because it has never been damaged by war.

European bison

Lake Bled bell

This is Lake Bled in Slovenia. Legend says that ringing the bell in the tower makes your wish come true.

Bison

About 1,000 wild bison live in Poland's forests. One of these enormous animals weighs as much as a family car.

Puppet performers

The Czechs love the theater. Puppet theater is especially popular here and in Slovakia.

What is the Czech word for "yes"?

Painted presents

Czechs and Slovaks give each other colored eggs at Easter. They are hard-boiled and painted by hand.

Dubrovnik's walled defenses.

Hot spring baths

Budapest is famous for its thermal baths. They are filled with hot water from underground springs. Bathing in the water is supposed to heal diseases.

Puppets

Dubrovnik

This ancient walled city is on the Croatian coast. Millions of people come here to walk the narrow streets and enjoy the cool sea air.

Eastern Europe

The countries of eastern Europe lie between the Baltic Sea and the Black Sea. They were part of the Soviet Union, but became independent states in 1991.

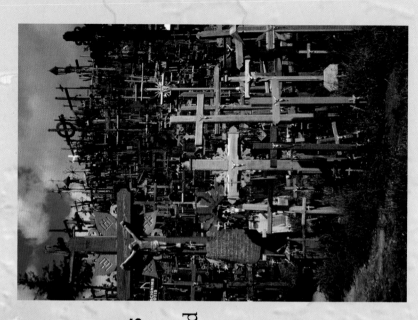

Hill of Crosses

This sacred site in Lithuania is visited by lots of pilgrims every year. They leave crosses on the hill to show their devotion to Christianity.

Russian Federation

Lake
Peipus

● TALLINN

Estonia

Golden
eagle

Bobsled

Latvian
costume

Vitsyebsk ●

● Polatsk

Cruise ship

RIGA ●

Latvia

● Bauska

The center
of Europe

VILNIUS ●

Lithuania

Flax

Belarus

MINSK ●

Amber jewelry

● Liepaja

Hill of Crosses

Trakai Castle

Sugar
beet

Pigs

Baltic Sea

Poland

What are the Baltic States?

N E W S

Coal mining
• Donets'k

Sea of Azov

• Kerch

Kharkiv •

White geese

Sunflowers

Crimea

Dnieper River

• Dnipropetrovs'k

• Yalta

St. Andrew's Church

Homyel •

• Chernihiv

Wheat

Mushroom-
picking

• KIEV

Black Sea
tourism

Swallow's
Nest
Castle

• Chernobyl

Wooden church

Odessa •

Black Sea

Ukraine

Mammoth
fossils

Gymnastic
school

Pripet Marshes

Mink

• CHISINAU

Moldova

Potatoes

Wooden
Moldovan
gateway

Ukrainian folk dancers

Chernivtsi •

• L'viy

Carpathian
Mountains

Romania

Can you find...

Ukraine's oldest creatures?
Mammoths lived on Earth
25,000 years ago.

The plant used to make linen?
Flax is a major crop of Belarus. Its
fibers are made into linen clothes.

Europe's largest marshland?
The Pripet Marshes cover 104,000 sq
miles (270,000 square kilometers).

Estonia, Latvia, and Lithuania—the countries bordering the Baltic Sea.

77

Eastern Europe

The cold Baltic Sea makes Estonia, Latvia, and Lithuania damp and chilly. Ukraine is rich in natural resources such as oil, gas, coal, and metal ores.

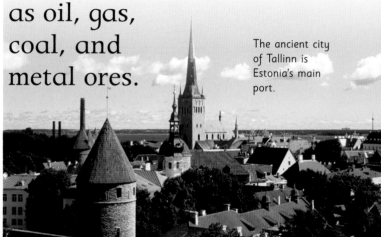

The ancient city of Tallinn is Estonia's main port.

Rural life
Modern industries are growing in eastern Europe, but many people still live off the land. Farmers work with hand tools and horses instead of machines and tractors.

Estonian capital
Only a million people live in the hilly, wet country of Estonia. A third of them live in the capital, Tallinn.

Rhythmic gymnasts twirl ribbons and hoops as they leap around.

Luge tracks are covered in ice.

Latvian luge
Near Riga in Latvia is a huge bobsled and luge track used for international races. Competitors hurtle down it at up to 78 mph (125 km/h).

Dancing gymnasts
Rhythmic gymnastics is a very popular sport in Ukraine. It is a combination of gymnastics and dance, set to music.

What is the world's most expensive caviar called?

Lithuanian amber

Amber is a kind of gem that forms over millions of years from conifer tree resin. Sometimes it has tiny creatures trapped inside it. Nearly all of the world's amber comes from mines in northern Lithuania.

This spider became trapped in amber millions of years ago.

Castle on the coast

One of the best-known sights in southern Ukraine is Swallow's Nest Castle on the coast of Crimea. It used to be the home of a German oil tycoon but is now an Italian restaurant.

Swallow's Nest Castle is perched on a cliff overlooking the Black Sea.

Wolves

Gray wolves have been killed off in most of Europe, but packs of wolves still roam free in the Carpathian Mountains in southwestern Ukraine. They hunt wild boar and deer in mountain forests.

Traditional food

These are some of the traditional dishes eaten in Eastern Europe.

Draniki is made from potato pancakes stuffed with meat.

Caviar is an expensive delicacy made from the eggs of sturgeon fish.

Borscht is beet soup. It is eaten hold or cold.

Black Sea tourism

Many Eastern Europeans and Russians spend their summer vacations in Crimea, which has warm weather, miles of beaches, and dramatic, hilly scenery.

Almas caviar. It is shimmering white and costs $9,500 per pound.

Southeast Europe

The mighty Danube River winds its way across southeast Europe, forming a natural border between Romania and Bulgaria. Farther south are the scattered ruins of the cities of ancient Greece.

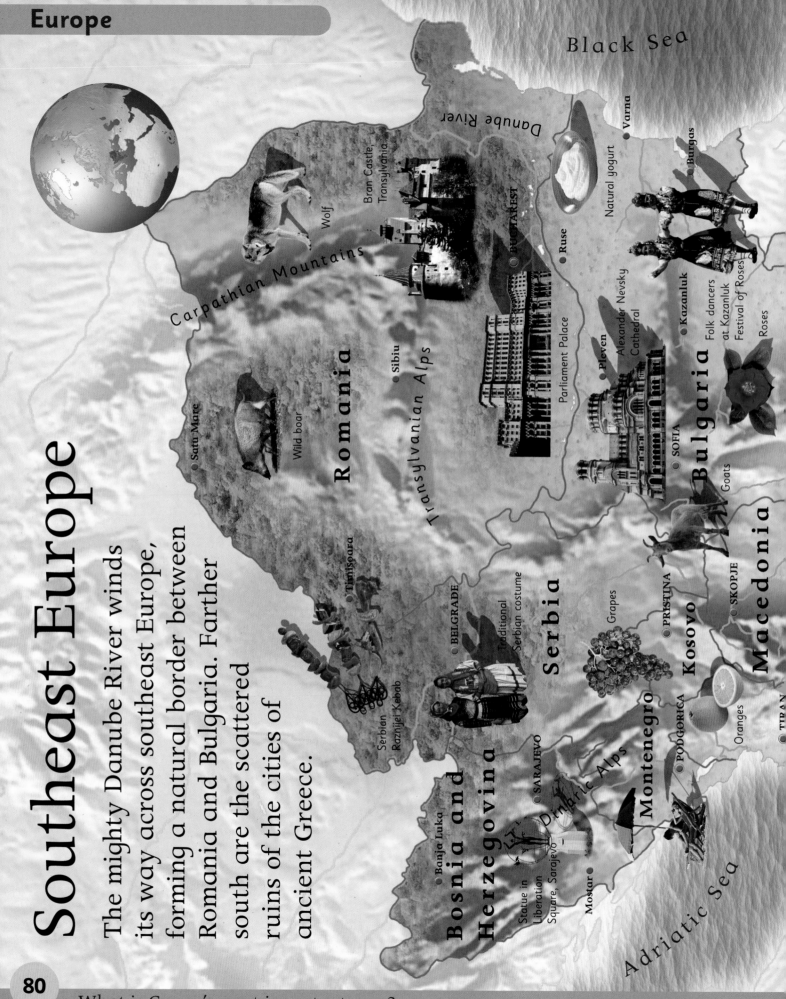

Black Sea

Danube River

Varna

Burgas

Natural yogurt

Bran Castle, Transylvania

Wolf

Carpathian Mountains

BUCHAREST

Ruse

Alexander Nevsky Cathedral

Pleven

Parliament Palace

Kazanluk

Folk dancers at Kazanluk Festival of Roses

Roses

Satu Mare

Wild boar

Romania

Sibiu

Transylvanian Alps

SOFIA

Bulgaria

Goats

Timișoara

BELGRADE

Traditional Serbian costume

Serbia

PRISTINA

SKOPJE

Kosovo

Macedonia

Grapes

Serbian Raznijel Kebab

Banja Luka

Bosnia and Herzegovina

SARAJEVO

Dinaric Alps

Montenegro

PODGORICA

Oranges

TIRAN

Statue in Liberation Square, Sarajevo

Mostar

Adriatic Sea

What is Greece's most important crop?

N
E
S
W

Turkey

Rhodes

Sponge

Lesbos

Chíos

Dolphins

Cyclades Islands

Knossos Palace

Iráklion
Crete

Aegean Sea

Bouzouki

ATHENS

Ceremonial soldier
from Athens

Salonika

Olive oil

Greece

Parthenon

Peloponnese

Patras

Mediterranean Sea

Bitola

Greek coffee

Pindus Mountains

Greek vase

Greek church

Albania

Cephalonia

Zakinthos

Watermelon

Sailing ship

Octopus

Can you find...

A sponge? Old-fashioned bathroom sponges are the skeletons of dead sea creatures.

Yogurt? People in Bulgaria eat lots of yogurt because they think it helps them live longer.

Greek coffee? Greek people make coffee by boiling ground coffee in a tiny pan of water until it foams.

Chíos Island in the Aegean Sea

Olives.

Southeast Europe

Southeast Europe is hot and hilly, with miles of sunny beaches. Many of the people are farmers, but the tourism is also important. People from all over the world visit Greece to see its ancient ruins and visit its islands.

Greek soldiers
This soldier is called an Evzone. He is a guard at the Greek parliament building in Athens.

Food
Many crops are grown in this part of Europe.

Grapes for making wine grow well in the warm climate.

Watermelons are refreshing fruits that grow on the ground.

Corn is grown for flour, animal food, and as a fuel.

The Parthenon
This ancient temple stands on a rocky outcrop in the center of Athens. It was built nearly 2,500 years ago.

White-washed churches dot the sunny islands of Greece.

Greek islands
Greece has more than 2,000 sun-baked islands. Millions of Europeans come here on vacation.

What major sporting tournament began in Greece in 776 BC?

Bran Castle,
Transylvania

Rose festival
Bulgarian farmers grow roses for making perfume. About 2,000 petals are needed to make just one gram (0.04 oz) of rose oil. The rose-pickers hold a festival every year at harvest time.

Rose-picking festival in June at Kazanluk, Bulgaria

The legend of Dracula
Transylvania is a region in northern Romania. The mountains here are covered with forests. Transylvania was the home of a vampire in the novel *Dracula*.

Goat farming
Farming is hard work in the dry heat of Greece. Many farmers keep a herd of goats for cheese and milk.

Dancing gypsy
Southeast Europe has many Romany people (gypsies). They spend their lives traveling, and they love traditional music and dance.

The Olympic Games.

83

Russia and Central Asia

The Russian Federation spans two continents: Europe and Asia. To its southwest are the eight countries of Central Asia and the Caucasus.

Barents Sea

Murmansk

Icebreaker ship

Harp seal

Kara Sea

Kaliningrad

St. Petersburg

Pskov

Novgorod

Vorkuta

Noril'sk

St. Basil's Cathedral, Moscow

MOSCOW

Kirov ballet

Kirov

Ob River

S i b

Ural Mountains

Russian dolls

Ob River

Volga River

Chess

Elk

Ural'sk

Magnitogorsk

R u s s i a n

Orsk

Omsk

Black Sea

Novosibirsk

Caucasus

Grozny

Sturgeon fish caviar

Baikonur Space Center

Wheat

Georgia

ASTANA

TBILISI

Baikonur

Zhezkazgan

YEREVAN

Armenia

Azerbaijan

Kazakhstan

BAKU

Lake Balkhash

Caspian Sea

Aral Sea

Uzbekistan

Kyzyl Kum Desert

Turkmenistan

Cotton

BISHKEK

TASHKENT

Almaty

Iran

ASHGABAT

Samarqand

Kyrgyzstan

Gur-Emir Mausoleum, Samarqand

DUSHANBE

Tajikistan

Afghanistan

Where is 90 percent of Russia's tea grown?

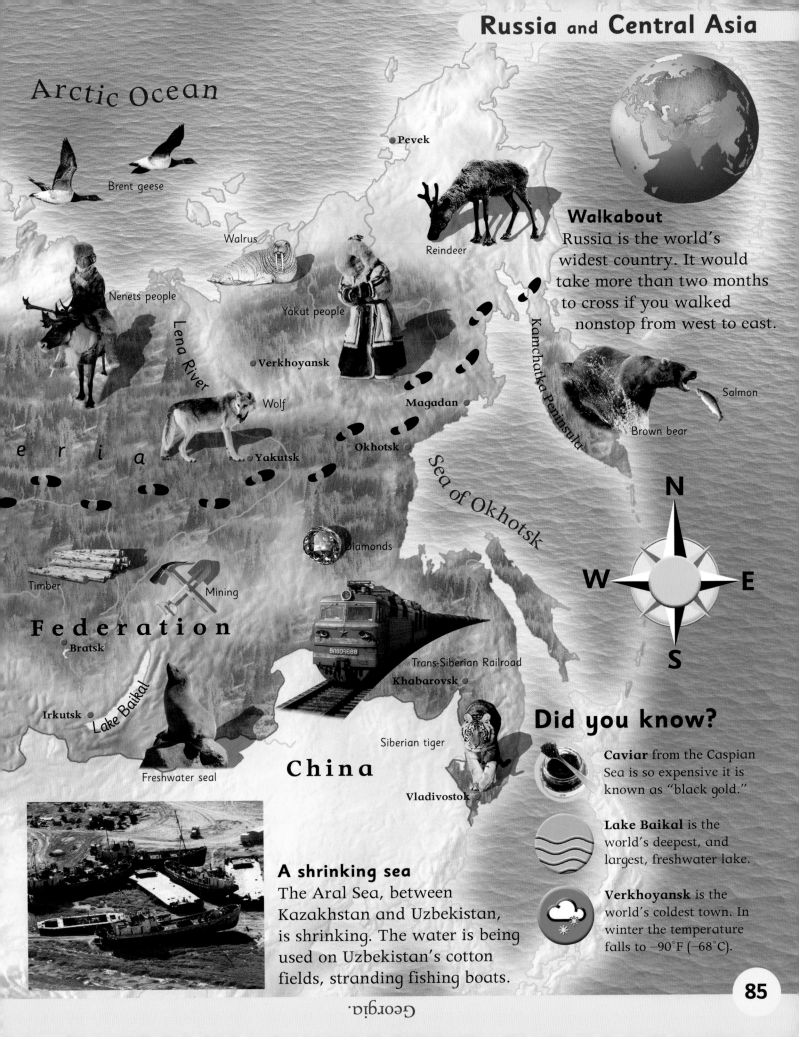

Arctic Ocean

Brent geese

Walrus

Nenets people

Lena River

Yakut people

Verkhoyansk

Wolf

Yakutsk

Okhotsk

Magadan

Pevek

Reindeer

Kamchatka Peninsula

Salmon

Brown bear

Walkabout
Russia is the world's widest country. It would take more than two months to cross if you walked nonstop from west to east.

Sea of Okhotsk

Diamonds

N
W **E**
S

Timber

Mining

F e d e r a t i o n

Bratsk

Irkutsk

Lake Baikal

Freshwater seal

Trans-Siberian Railroad

Khabarovsk

Siberian tiger

C h i n a

Vladivostok

Did you know?

Caviar from the Caspian Sea is so expensive it is known as "black gold."

Lake Baikal is the world's deepest, and largest, freshwater lake.

Verkhoyansk is the world's coldest town. In winter the temperature falls to –90°F (–68°C).

A shrinking sea
The Aral Sea, between Kazakhstan and Uzbekistan, is shrinking. The water is being used on Uzbekistan's cotton fields, stranding fishing boats.

Russia

Russia is the world's largest country. Most people live in cities in the west, near the rest of Europe. Russia is governed from Moscow.

The Summer Palace
This magnificent palace is in St. Petersburg. It was built 300 years ago for Peter the Great, who was the czar, or ruler, of Russia.

Russian churches have domed roofs shaped like onions.

St. Basil's

St. Basil's Cathedral is in Red Square, Moscow. Churches are important to Russians. Three-fourths of Russians follow the Russian Orthodox branch of Christianity.

Russian dolls fit inside each other.

What was St. Petersburg called when Russia was in the Soviet Union?

Ballet school

The Bolshoi Ballet is Russia's most famous ballet company. Dancers trained at its ballet school perform at the Bolshoi Theater in Moscow.

Russian culture

Culture is very important in Russia, especially music, art, theater, and literature.

Tchaikovsky and **Stravinsky**, both famous composers, were born in Russia.

The Russian writer **Tolstoy** wrote the famous novel *War and Peace*.

The **balalaika** is a traditional Russian instrument. It is played by plucking its strings.

Soviet Russia

Russia once belonged to a huge federation called the Soviet Union. The Kremlin in Moscow was its seat of government.

The Kremlin is an enormous fortress in Moscow.

The red star, hammer, and sickle were the symbols of the Soviet Union.

Brown bear

The brown bear is the symbol of Russia. It lives in the north, hunting fish and small animals.

Vladimir Ilyich Lenin (1870–1924) was the leader who founded the Soviet Union.

Leningrad.

Siberia and neighbors

Siberia is a vast area of pine forests to the east of the Ural mountains. Northern Siberia is so cold that the ground is frozen year-round.

Reindeer
This ivory carving from Siberia shows a reindeer pulling a sled. People in northern Siberia keep reindeer for milk, meat, and fur, as well as for pulling sleds.

Tents of Siberian reindeer herders

Siberian people
The Nenets live in the forests of Siberia in winter. In summer they pack up their tents and travel north with reindeer herds to pasture in the Arctic.

Nenets children wear fur coats and fur-lined boots.

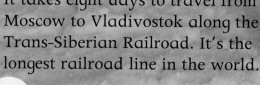

The Trans-Siberian Railroad
It takes eight days to travel from Moscow to Vladivostok along the Trans-Siberian Railroad. It's the longest railroad line in the world.

How long is the Trans-Siberian Railroad?

Oil in Azerbaijan

There is a lot of oil, gas, coal, and other materials under the ground in Azerbaijan in Central Asia. Azerbaijan gets most of its money by selling oil.

Made in Russia

Here are some of the well-known objects made by Russia's craftspeople.

 A **samovar** is a decorated urn for heating water for tea.

 Antique jewelry **Fabergé eggs** are worth a fortune.

 Clay dolls have been made for the Dymkovo village fair for many years.

 Warm **boots** are made from the furs of Siberian forest animals.

 Many Russian **toys** were traditionally carved from wood.

Russian Rockets

Baikonur Space Center in Kazakhstan is the home of Russia's space program, and where they launch their rockets. Sputnik, the first man-made space satellite, was launched here in 1957.

The top of the rocket carries a satellite or supplies for astronauts already in space.

Engines push the rocket upward.

Rockets lift off from Baikonur Space Center.

Weaving carpets

Central Asian women weave decorative woolen carpets to give as wedding presents. The carpets are made by hand and colored with plant dyes.

5,870 miles (9,440 km).

Middle East

This part of the world is hot and dry, with large deserts. Three of the world's great religions began here.

Mediterranean Sea

Istanbul

Blue Mosque   ANKARA

Turkey

NICOSIA
Cyprus

Sculpted menorah in Jerusalem

Mecca

The holiest place for a Muslim is the Ka'ba, a cube-shaped shrine in Mecca. Muslims face the Ka'ba when they pray and try to visit it at least once in their lifetime.

World's first skyscrapers

The people of Yemen started building mud-brick skyscrapers thousands of years ago. The ground floors are used for animals or for storing goods. Families live in the upper floors.

Fruits of the desert

Farmers can grow crops only in the wettest parts of the Middle East.

 Figs are soft, sticky fruits that can be dried to make them last longer.

 Olives are grown for their seeds, which are pressed to make olive oil.

 Dates are the fruit of palm trees, which grow by rivers and in oases.

Which country produces 65 percent of the world's hazelnuts?

Black Sea

Caspian Sea

Whirling dervish dance

Head of Zeus

Mount Ararat
16,945 ft ▲
(5,165 m)

Syria

Olives

BEIRUT

Figs

DAMASCUS

Lebanon

AMMAN

JERUSALEM

Jordan

Israel

Iraq

BAGHDAD

Marsh Arab reed house

TEHRAN

Turquoise

Iran

Chador, traditional dress for women

Iranian food—chicken kebab

Ancient city of Petra

Falconry

Desert oasis

Kuwait

KUWAIT CITY

Persian Gulf

Persepolis palace

Mecca

RIYADH

Oil

Bahrain

Qatar

DOHA

ABU DHABI

Oman

Gulf of Oman

MUSCAT

Oil refinery

Saudi Arabia

United Arab Emirates

Arabian Desert

Red Sea

Coral reefs grow along the coast of the Red Sea, where the water is warm and clear.

Mecca

Camels

Desert oryx

Oman

Yemen

Frankincense tree

SANA

Oil tanker

Arabian Sea

N
W   E
S

Middle East

The Middle East lies at the crossroads between Europe, Africa, and Asia. Most of the people are Muslims—followers of the religion of Islam.

Middle Eastern treat

Baklava is a popular Middle Eastern pastry. It is made from rolled layers of thin pastry and chopped nuts, covered with sticky honey.

The towers around a mosque are called minarets. This is the Blue Mosque in Istanbul, Turkey.

Patterned Islamic tile

Mosques

Muslims pray in buildings called mosques. Mosques are decorated with patterned tiles and verses from the Muslim holy book, the Koran.

Traditional dress

Muslim women hide their hair and the shape of their body with loose-fitting clothes when they go out in public.

Camels can last for ten months

Camel train carrying cargo across the desert

What language is spoken in most of the Middle East?

The Western Wall
Jerusalem is a holy city for Muslims, Christians, and Jews. Jews pray at the Western Wall. It is the only part that is left of a Jewish temple that was built 2,000 years ago.

Oil wealth
More than half the world's oil lies under the ground in the Middle East. The discovery of oil and gas has made many of the countries in the Middle East very rich. They sell lots of oil to other countries, some of which is turned into gasoline for cars.

Salty sea
The Dead Sea is 1,300 ft (400 meters) below sea level. It is so salty that people can float in the water. Plants and animals cannot survive in it.

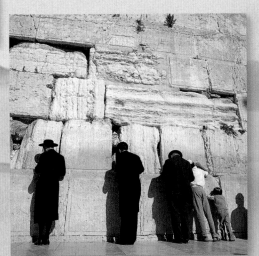

Burj-Al-Arab hotel in Dubai, United Arab Emirates

World's tallest hotel
The Burj-Al-Arab hotel in Dubai is the world's tallest hotel. It was built on an artificial island and designed to look like the sail of a ship.

get going
Make an Arab headdress. Fold a checkered tablecloth diagonally in half and hang it over your head, leaving your face clear. Then tie it in place with a dark belt or ribbon.

Arab men wear long, baggy clothes and a headdress to shade them from the hot desert sun.

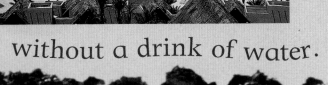

without a drink of water.

Southern Asia

Southern Asia is colorful and crowded. India is the biggest country in the region, with a population of more than a billion.

Elephants on parade

During the festival of Puram in southern India, 101 elephants march through the town of Trichur in a grand parade.

Snow leopard

Afghanistan

Herat

Lapis lazuli

Decorated truck

KABUL

Pakistan

Tomb of Muhammad Ali Jinnah

Karachi

Quetta

Dancer

ISLAMABAD

Multan

Hyderabad

Golden Temple

Taj Mahal

Delhi
NEW DELHI

Agra

India

Camel market

Surat

Narmada River

Rickshaw

Nepal

Ganges River

River dolphin

Sacred cow

Bangladesh

DHAKA

Calcutta

Chittagong

Imphal

Tea-picking

Green turtles

When Hindus die, where are their ashes scattered?

Coconut tree and coconut

Bay of Bengal

Cuttack

Andaman Islands (India)

Fishing boat

Nicobar Islands (India)

N
E
W
S

Raipur

Common lobster

Nagpur

Tiger

Vijayawada

Herring

Chennai (Madras)

Thresher shark

Mumbai (Bombay)

Snake-charmer

Sri Lanka

Jaffna

Kandy

Tea leaves

Indian elephant

Kathkali Dancer

Calicut

Trichur

COLOMBO

The Monsoon

Southern Asia is normally hot and dry, but each summer rain pours down for weeks. This rainy season, called the monsoon, helps farmers grow crops like rice.

Arabian Sea

Tuna fish

Can you find...

Lapis lazuli? This precious stone was once used to make brilliant, sky blue paint.

An Indian dancer? Classical dancers use movements of their bodies to tell ancient stories.

Ganges river dolphin? This dolphin is almost blind and finds its way in muddy water by sound.

In the Ganges River.

Southern Asia

Different cultures and religions mix together in Southern Asia. Most people are Hindus, but there are also Muslims, Buddhists, Sikhs, and Christians.

Indian food

Traditional Indian meals consist of lots of separate dishes on a metal plate called a thali.

Spicy chicken

Dumplings

Lentil soup

Vegetables

Bread

Rice

Raita (yogurt dip)

Poppadoms

Pilgrims bathing in the Ganges

Disappearing tigers

Tigers once lived all over southern Asia, but today they are rare because of hunting. Parts of India and Bangladesh still have man-eating tigers.

Four minarets surround the central tomb.

Indian arts

Indian people enjoy music, dance, theater, and storytelling. In the art of Kathakali, dancers act out Hindu myths.

Kathakali dancer

The Holy Ganges

The Ganges River is sacred to Hindus. They believe that the river's water washes away their sins. Millions of pilgrims bathe at the holy city of Varanasi.

What is the main crop in Sri Lanka?

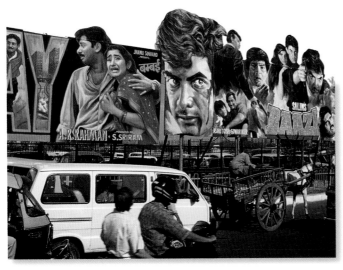

Bollywood

So many films are made in Bombay (Mumbai) that people call this town Bollywood. Indian movies are very long and feature lots of singing and dancing.

The elephant god Ganesh

Taj Mahal

The Taj Mahal is a tomb. An Indian emperor called Shah Jahan built it more than 300 years ago for his favorite wife when she died.

Hindu gods

Hindus worship many gods. Statues of Ganesh, the elephant god, are placed near entrances to houses.

get going

Make some raita (Indian yogurt dip). Put some plain yogurt in a small dish. Grate some cucumber and mix it into the yogurt. Add a sprinkling of cilantro leaves or mint.

Tea.

Southeast Asia

Southeast Asia is hot and rainy all year. There are thousands of islands, and many are covered with steamy rainforests and towering volcanoes.

China

Elephant

Myanmar (Burma)

Thai dancer

NAY PYI TAW

Rubies

HANOI

Laos

VIENTIANE

Yangon

Thailand

Vietnam

Sampan boat

BANGKOK

Angkor Wat

Tapir

Cambodia

South China Sea

PHNOM PENH

Ho Chi Minh

Pearls

Floating market

The city of Bangkok is crisscrossed with canals. Traders sell their goods from boats and shoppers paddle by to look for bargains.

Orchid

Petronas Towers

Omar Ali Saifuddin Mosque

Brunei

BANDAR SERI BEGAWA

Tiger

KUALA LUMPUR

M a l a y s i a

Singapore

Orangutan

S u m a t r a

Padang

I n d

B o r n e o

Coconu

Rafflesia (giant flower)

o

JAKARTA

J a v a

Shadow puppets

What is the largest lizard in the world?

Can you find...

A very rare kind of ape? **Orangutans** live only in Borneo and Sumatra.

An animal with tusks that grow through its face? The **babirusa** is a kind of pig.

The world's largest flower? **Rafflesia** grows to nearly a yard (meter) wide.

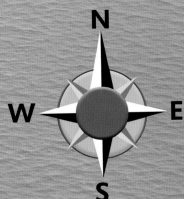

MANILA

Planting rice

Vinta boats

Philippines

Cebu

Water buffalo

Davao

Pacific Ocean

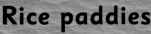
Tuna

Celebes Sea

Babirusa

Celebes

Toraja house

n e s i a

Moluccas

Nutmeg

Ambon

Rice paddies

The wet climate is ideal for growing rice. Farmers plant it in flooded fields called paddies, which are sometimes built like steps in the sides of hills.

Jayapura

N e w   G u i n e a

Conch shell

Papua New Guinea

Asmat warrior

PORT MORESBY

Komodo dragon

DILI

East Timor

Mangoes

The Komodo dragon. It can grow to 10 ft (3 m) long.

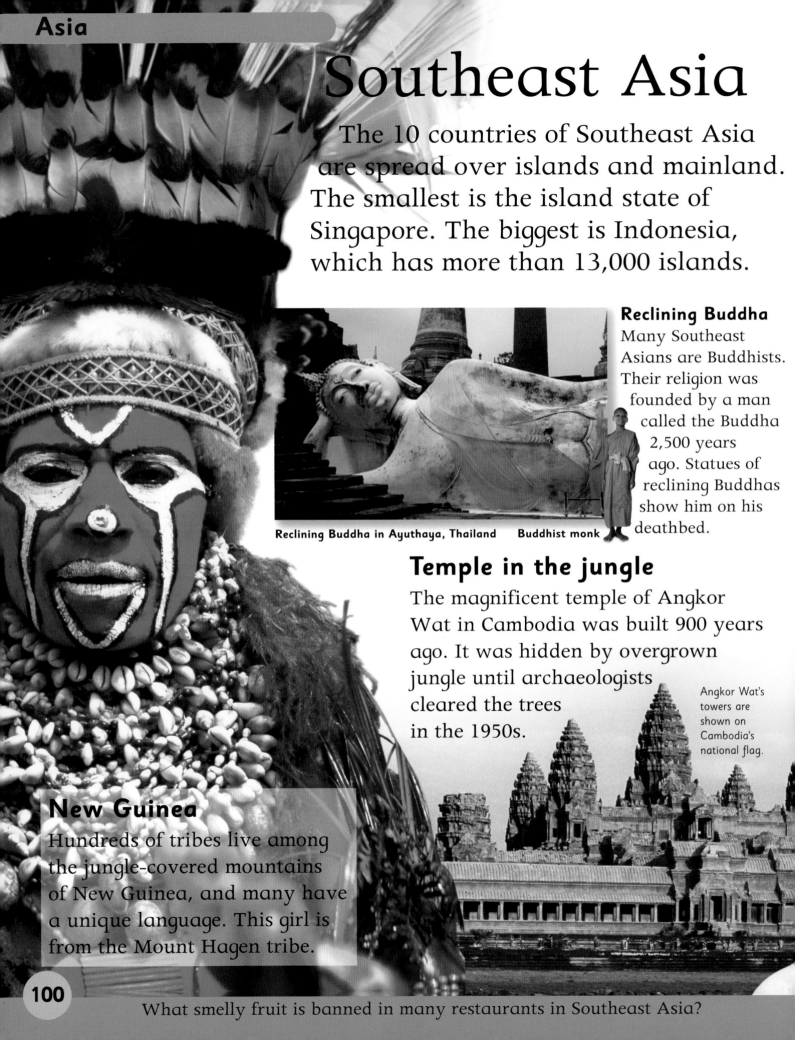

Southeast Asia

The 10 countries of Southeast Asia are spread over islands and mainland. The smallest is the island state of Singapore. The biggest is Indonesia, which has more than 13,000 islands.

Reclining Buddha

Many Southeast Asians are Buddhists. Their religion was founded by a man called the Buddha 2,500 years ago. Statues of reclining Buddhas show him on his deathbed.

Reclining Buddha in Ayuthaya, Thailand   Buddhist monk

Temple in the jungle

The magnificent temple of Angkor Wat in Cambodia was built 900 years ago. It was hidden by overgrown jungle until archaeologists cleared the trees in the 1950s.

Angkor Wat's towers are shown on Cambodia's national flag.

New Guinea

Hundreds of tribes live among the jungle-covered mountains of New Guinea, and many have a unique language. This girl is from the Mount Hagen tribe.

What smelly fruit is banned in many restaurants in Southeast Asia?

Exotic Fruit

Tropical fruits grow well in Southeast Asia's warm, wet climate.

 The **durian** tastes delicious but smells disgusting.

 Inside a **coconut** is white flesh and a hole filled with liquid.

 The **custard apple** has cream-colored flesh like thick custard.

 Slices of **starfruit** make star-shaped decorations for desserts.

 The **rambutan** has a tough skin covered with soft hairs.

The Petronas Towers
These office buildings in Kuala Lumpur, Malaysia, were the world's tallest buildings from 1998 until 2003. Each tower is 1,483 ft (452 m) tall.

Island wildlife
Many extraordinary animals and plants live in Southeast Asia. Orangutans live in rainforests on Borneo and Sumatra. Komodo dragons are flesh-eating lizards found on a few islands in Indonesia.

Long-necked women
The Karen tribe live in the hills of Burma. The women stretch their necks as they grow up by wearing neck rings.

Orangutans swing on flimsy trees and branches to move through the forest.

Komodo dragon

China and neighbors

Over 1 billion people live in China; that's one-fifth of the world's people. Next door, Mongolia has the fewest people for its size.

Terracotta Army

This army of statues in Xi'an was made more than 2,000 years ago to guard the tomb of Qin Shi Huang, China's first emperor. The statues were rediscovered in 1974.

Chinese opera

Chinese opera has lots of singing, acting, and acrobatics. Makeup is used to show the type of character being played.

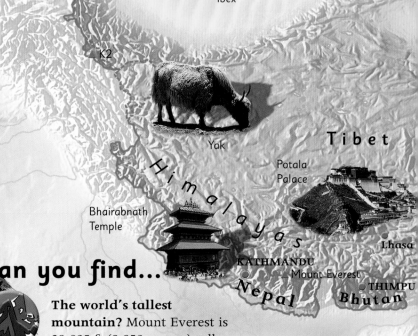

N
W — E
S

Altay

Mongolian ger (house)

Yining

Urumqi

Bactrian camel

Turpan

Hami

Kashi

Ibex

K2

Yak

Tibet

Potala Palace

Himalayas

Lhasa

Bhairabnath Temple

KATHMANDU

Mount Everest

Nepal

THIMPU

Bhutan

Can you find...

The world's tallest mountain? Mount Everest is 29,035 ft (8,850 meters) tall.

The world's most crowded place? Hong Kong has 2,300 people per square mile (6,000 per square kilometer).

China's hottest place? Turpan has recorded temperatures of up to 117°F (47°C).

102

What is the world's second-tallest mountain?

Russian Federation

Mongolia

ULAN BATOR

Dinosaur fossils

Gobi Desert

Harbin

Snow sculptures at the
Harbin Ice Festival

Jinlin

Shenyang

North Korea

PYONGYANG

Dalian

SEOUL

South
Korea

Seoul
Olympic
Stadium

Temple of Heaven

BEIJING

Qingdao

Korea
Strait

Great Wall of China

China

Tibetan
monk

Lanzhou

Xi'an

Yellow River

Tea plantation

Yangtze River

Wuhan

East China
Sea

Shanghai

Hanzhou

Junk (fishing boat)

Chengdu

China porcelain

Changsha

Silk moth

Fuzhou

TAIPEI

Taiwan

Red panda

Kunming

Giant panda

Hong Kong business
district and Exhibition
Center

Hong Kong

Electronic
goods

Nanning

Hainan

South China Sea

K2 in the Himalayas. It is 28,250 ft (8,611 meters) tall.

Eastern China and Korea

China is a vast and ancient country. Emperors ruled it for thousands of years, but today it has a communist government. Korea is split into two countries: North Korea and South Korea.

Packed Hong Kong

Hong Kong is a small and crowded region of China. It is an important center for banking and commerce.

Staple food

Rice is the main crop, and the most important source of food, in China and Korea. Eastern China's rainy climate is ideal for rice, which grows best in flooded fields.

Rice is eaten with chopsticks.

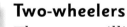

Rice farm

Great Wall

More than 500 years ago, the Chinese built the Great Wall of China to keep out invaders from Mongolia. It is the longest man-made structure in the world.

Two-wheelers

There are millions of bicycles in China, especially in rural areas. In cities such as Beijing, there are more cars. Bicycles are also used as taxis or as market stands.

What are Chinese years named after?

Martial arts

Chinese and Korean people have turned fighting into an art form. One of the most popular martial arts in Korea is tae kwon do, which is used for self-defense or sport. Kicking and punching are allowed.

Tae kwon do fighters

The misty Guilin mountains are said to be the most beautiful place in China.

Chinese New Year

The most important festival in China is the Chinese New Year, when people celebrate the return of spring. One of the main events is a parade led by a huge dancing dragon.

The Chinese dragon is a symbol of strength and good luck.

Guilin Mountains

The town of Guilin in southern China is surrounded by small, pointy mountains that are often shrouded in mist. They are a favorite subject for Chinese painters.

Himalayas and Western China

The Himalayas are the tallest mountains on Earth, yet many people live among them. North of the mountains are the cold, dusty highlands of western China and Mongolia.

Monks and prayer wheels

Tibetan monks
In Tibet, Buddhist monks start their training as young boys. They shave their heads, wear red robes, and join a monastery for life.

The Himalayan peaks are always snowy.

The Himalayas stretch for 1,550 miles (2,500 km).

Mountain villages
In Nepal, villages are dotted around in valleys between the highest mountains. Farmers build flat terraces in the hillsides for growing crops.

Who is the Dalai Lama?

Mongolian horsemen

Mongolians learn to ride by the age of three. Many spend their lives on the move, riding across Mongolia's vast plains with herds of horses and sheep.

Mongolian horse-riding festival

Climbing Everest

The ultimate challenge for a mountaineer is to climb Mount Everest, the world's tallest mountain. Dozens of people reach the summit every year, but some die on the way.

Climbing Mount Everest is exhausting and dangerous.

Buddhist prayer flags.

get going

Make Buddhist prayer flags. Attach squares of colored tissue paper to a length of string. Hang the string across your room or your yard.

Potala Palace

In the town of Lhasa in Tibet stands a mighty fortress called Potala Palace. It used to be the headquarters of the Tibetan government before Tibet became a part of China.

The useful yak

A yak is kind of huge, shaggy cow that can survive in the cold, thin mountain air. Tibetan people get milk, butter, meat, and wool from yaks.

Basket hangs on back.

Cheese sellers

These Tibetan girls are nomads, which means they move from place to place. They are selling dried yak's cheese.

The head of Tibetan Buddhism and the leader of Tibet's people.

Kurile Islands

Japan

Japan is made up of four large islands and several thousand small ones. Most of the country is mountainous. The biggest cities are near the coast, where the land is flat.

Steller's sea eagle

Japanese crane

Hokkaido

Pollock

Snow monkey

Sapporo

Apples

Aomori

Sushi

Cups for rice wine

Ou Mountains

Honshu

Sea of Japan

Snow and ice festival

An ice festival takes place every February in the town of Sapporo. People carve towers of ice into temples, sculptures, or replicas of famous buildings.

How many people live in Tokyo?

Toys and gadgets

Japan makes lots of electronic goods, such as computer games, televisions, and robot pets.

Robot dog

Kabuki theater

TOKYO

Izu Islands

Ogasawara Islands

Volcano Islands

Mount Fuji 12,388 ft (3,776 m)

Nagoya

Nagoya Castle

Pearl in shell

Pacific Ocean

Osaka

Kyoto

Chugoku Mountains

Bullet train

Tokyo skyline

The capital city of Tokyo is crowded and lively. Its skyscrapers are designed to sway slightly, which protects them from falling during earthquakes.

Geishas

Oki Islands

Shinto shrine

Hiroshima

Shikoku

Matsuyama Castle

Sumo wrestlers

Kyushu

Iki

Fukuoka

Bonsai tree

Pottery

Nagasaki

Sakishima Islands

These small tropical islands lie far to the south of the rest of Japan.

Ishigaki

Iriomote

Yonaguni

Octopus

East China Sea

Ryukyu Islands

Okinawa

Japan

Japan is a fascinating mixture of old and new. Its people work very hard and have made Japan very wealthy.

Cherry blossom

Mount Fuji

Mount Fuji

This snow-capped volcano is the symbol of Japan, and many Japanese people have a picture of it in their homes. Mount Fuji last erupted in 1707.

Snow monkeys
Japanese macaques stay warm in winter by bathing in hot springs. These clever monkeys have also learned to make snowballs.

Bullet trains
Japanese "bullet trains" are among the fastest trains in the world. They shoot between cities at up to 167 mph (270 km/h).

Volcano protection
Volcanoes and earthquakes are common in Japan. In the city of Kagoshima, children wear helmets to protect them from rocks and ash from nearby Mount Sakurajima.

What do Japanese people call their country?

Traditional dress

On special occasions, women and girls wear a kimono—a richly embroidered silk dress tied with a sash.

Cherry blossom

The national flower of Japan is the cherry blossom. In spring, people celebrate the arrival of the cherry blossom with picnics under the trees.

Sumo

Traditional Japanese wrestling is called sumo. The heavy wrestlers try to throw each other out of the ring, called the dohyo.

Thick belt called a mawashi.

Open shoes called zori.

Buddhist temple

Japan's two main religions are Buddhism and Shinto. Buddhist temples, or pagodas, consist of a stack of wooden floors and curved roofs. Ornate gardens often surround them.

Chopsticks

Sushi

Japanese people eat a lot of seafood. Sushi consists of small snacks of rice, raw fish, and vegetables.

Nippon or "the land of the rising Sun."

Australia

Australia is the world's smallest continent, but it is a huge country. Most Australians live on the coast, far from the vast, dusty deserts that make up the outback.

Poisonous animals

More poisonous animals live in Australia than in any other country.

The male **platypus** has a poisonous spur on each of its back ankles.

A **box jellyfish's** stings can kill and cause terrible pain that lasts for weeks.

Taipans are the world's deadliest snakes. A bite can kill in 30 minutes.

Sea snake venom can kill a child, but bites from these shy snakes are rare.

Cone shells are sea snails with deadly stingers. The venom causes suffocation.

Funnel-web spiders can bite through a fingernail and stop a person's heart.

The tiny **blue-ringed octopus** can paralyze and kill a person with its bite.

Darwin

Saltwater crocodile

Boomerang

Broome

Dingo

Tanami Desert

Great Sandy Desert

Northern Territory

Port Hedland

Emu

Iron ore

Road train

Camel

Musgrave

Western Australia

Great Victoria Desert

South Australia

Geraldton

Kalgoorlie

Perth skyline

Perth

Fremantle

Kangaroo

Esperance

Great Australian Bight

Great white shark

Albany

N
W   E
S

What is a coral reef made from?

Aboriginal paintings

Gulf of Carpentaria

Cape York Peninsula

Coral reef

The Great Barrier Reef stretches for 1,200 miles (2,000 km) along Queensland's coast. Many brightly colored fish live on the reef.

Cairns

Cattle farms

Tennant Creek

The Devils Marbles

Mount Isa

Townsville

Mackay

Rainbow lorikeet

Great Barrier Reef

Flying doctor

Queensland

Rockhampton

Great Dividing Range

Alice Springs

Simpson Desert

Sheep stations

Koala

Uluru (Ayers Rock)

Ranges

Lake Eyre

Banana plantations

Pineapple farms

Brisbane

Opals
Coober Pedy

Broken Hill

Funnel-web spider

Sydney Opera House

Port Augusta

New South Wales

Sydney

Wollongong

Whyalla

Kookaburra

Wagga Wagga

Adelaide

Murray river

Port Lincoln

CANBERRA

Australian Capital Territory

Kangaroo Island

Victoria

Mount Gambier

Melbourne

Tram

Bass Strait

Tasmanian devil

Tasmania

Hobart

Sailing

The skeletons of tiny sea creatures.

113

Australia

Australia is on the opposite side of the world from Europe, but most Australians are descended from European settlers. English is the main language in Australia.

Australian shepherds use jeeps to round up their enormous flocks.

Australian Aboriginals

The Aboriginals have lived in Australia for more than 50,000 years. According to their legends, the world was made by mythical beasts who carved the land into rivers and mountains.

Sheep farms

About a quarter of the world's wool comes from Australia. Some sheep farms are so remote that farmers need planes to visit town.

Boomerangs fly back to you after you throw them.

A boomerang is a throwing weapon that Aboriginals use for hunting.

What is the capital of Australia?

Gum trees (eucalyptus trees) have waxy, strong-smelling leaves.

Sydney

Australia's biggest city and chief port is Sydney. Its most famous building is Sydney Opera House in the harbor. Around Sydney are miles of beaches where children can swim and surf after school.

Koala

The only animal that can eat the leaves of Australia's gum trees is the koala. Koalas are very lazy and spend up to 20 hours a day sleeping.

get going

Make an Aboriginal lucky stone. Find a smooth, round pebble and paint a pattern of lines and dots on it to make a picture of an imaginary creature.

On the beach

In Australia, the seasons are the other way around. December is the middle of summer, so Australians celebrate Christmas on the beach.

Bouncing babies

Kangaroos are marsupials—they carry their babies in a pouch. Lots of Australian animals are marsupials.

Kangaroos move by hopping on their huge back feet.

Uluru

Uluru, or Ayers Rock, is a huge lump of sandstone rock in the center of Australia. Aboriginals believe it is a magical place.

New Zealand and the Pacific

Hundreds of islands are scattered across the Pacific Ocean. Two of the biggest form the mountainous country of New Zealand.

Extreme sports

New Zealand is the world capital for extreme sports. Bungee jumping, skydiving, and white-water rafting are all popular.

Maori war dance

Most people in New Zealand are European, but about one in ten are Maoris—New Zealand's native people. On special occasions, Maoris paint their faces and perform a war dance called a haka.

Moving house

Earthquakes are common in New Zealand, so people live in wooden houses for safety. When people move, they can carry their house away on a truck.

Sheep shearing

Kiwi

South Island

Mount Cook

Christchurch

Southern Alps

Takahe

Rugby

New

Queenstown

Dunedin

Bungee jumping

Royal albatross

Sheep

Oysters

What's unusual about New Zealand's kiwi birds?

Red snapper

N
W E
S

Auckland

Pohuto
geyser

Maori carving

Kiwi fruit

North Island

Parliament buildings
(Wellington)

WELLINGTON

Cook Strait

Zealand

Pacific
Ocean

Coconut palms
Forests of coconut palms
grow along the beaches
of the Pacific islands.
Islanders climb these tall
trees to gather the coconuts.

Pacific islands
About 5 million people live
among the tropical islands
of the central Pacific.

Northern Mariana
Islands (US)

Marshall
Islands

Guam (US)

Palau

Micronesia

Sperm
whale

Papua New
Guinea

Nauru

Kiribati

Solomon
Islands

Tuvalu

Tokelau (NZ)

Wallis &
Futuna
(France)

Samoa

American
Samoa
(US)

Pacific
islanders fish
from small
wooden canoes

Vanuatu

Tonga

Niue
(NZ)

Cook Islands
(NZ)

New
Caledonia
(France)

Fiji

French
Polynesia
(France)

They can't fly.

Antarctica

The world's coldest continent is Antarctica, which is covered in ice. In winter it doubles in size as the sea freezes around it.

Southern Ocean

Adélie penguins

Weddell Sea

South polar skua

Halley Research Station (UK)

Antarctic Peninsula

Ronne Ice Shelf

Penguins

Lots of sea animals live around Antarctica's coast. Penguins are clumsy on land but superb swimmers underwater.

Ellsworth Land

NORTH POLE 11708 MI.

CHRISTCHURCH 2,457 MI.

A signpost in Antarctica shows how far away the rest of the world is.

SEATTLE, WASH. 9,942 MI.

QUONSET PT. 10,598 MI.

ST. PAUL, MINN. 10,002 MI.

SOUTH POLE 831 MI.

Krill

Emperor penguins

SALINAS, CAL. 8,777 MI.

HOUSTON, TEXAS 9,141 MI.

MOBILE, ALA. 9,641 MI.

PONTIAC, MICH. 10,249 MI.

ERECTED BY YX-6 OF 3" WINTERING PARTY 1958 THEY WENT THAT-A-WAY ➤

Blue whale

Icebreaker

Scott and the Antarctic

The British explorer Robert Scott was one of the first people to reach the South Pole, in 1912. He died of cold and hunger on the way home.

Antarctic Circle

Southern Ocean

Who was the first person to reach the South Pole?

Right whale

Southern Ocean

Dronning Maud Land

Molodezhnaya Station (Russian Federation)

Survey plane

Adélie penguins

Antarctica

Princess Elizabeth Land

Amundsen-Scott Station (US), South Pole

● SOUTH POLE

Snowmobile

Transantarctic Mountains

Elephant seal

Vostok Station (Russian Federation)

Ross Ice Shelf

Casey Base (Australia)

McMurdo Air Station (US)

Ross Sea

Sno-cat

Dumont d'Urville (France)

Snow petrel

Killer whale

Antarctic science
The only people who live in Antarctica are scientists. They use huge balloons to study the climate of Antarctica.

Weather balloon.

Life in the freezer
Antarctica is so cold that it freezes your breath into icicles around your mouth. People have to cover up with lots of very warm clothes.

Icicles from breath.

The Norwegian explorer Roald Amundsen, in 1911.

Reference Section

Flags of the World

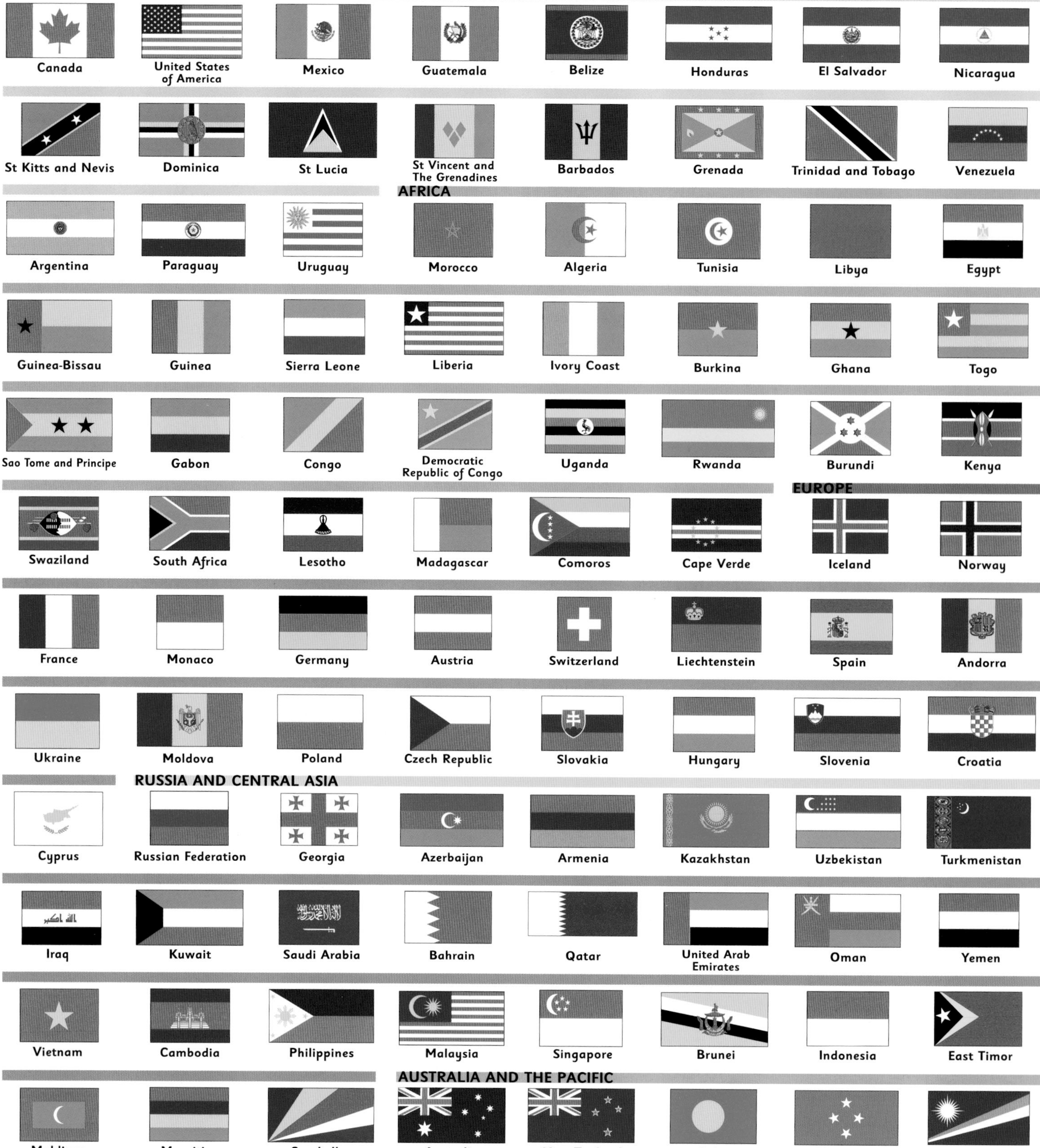

NORTH AND SOUTH AMERICA

Canada, United States of America, Mexico, Guatemala, Belize, Honduras, El Salvador, Nicaragua

St Kitts and Nevis, Dominica, St Lucia, St Vincent and The Grenadines, Barbados, Grenada, Trinidad and Tobago, Venezuela

Argentina, Paraguay, Uruguay

AFRICA

Morocco, Algeria, Tunisia, Libya, Egypt

Guinea-Bissau, Guinea, Sierra Leone, Liberia, Ivory Coast, Burkina, Ghana, Togo

Sao Tome and Principe, Gabon, Congo, Democratic Republic of Congo, Uganda, Rwanda, Burundi, Kenya

Swaziland, South Africa, Lesotho, Madagascar, Comoros, Cape Verde

EUROPE

Iceland, Norway

France, Monaco, Germany, Austria, Switzerland, Liechtenstein, Spain, Andorra

Ukraine, Moldova, Poland, Czech Republic, Slovakia, Hungary, Slovenia, Croatia

Cyprus

RUSSIA AND CENTRAL ASIA

Russian Federation, Georgia, Azerbaijan, Armenia, Kazakhstan, Uzbekistan, Turkmenistan

Iraq, Kuwait, Saudi Arabia, Bahrain, Qatar, United Arab Emirates, Oman, Yemen

Vietnam, Cambodia, Philippines, Malaysia, Singapore, Brunei, Indonesia, East Timor

Maldives, Mauritius, Seychelles

AUSTRALIA AND THE PACIFIC

Australia, New Zealand, Palau, Micronesia, Marshall Islands

Which is the only country that doesn't have a rectangular flag?

There are 196 countries in the world. Each has its own flag.

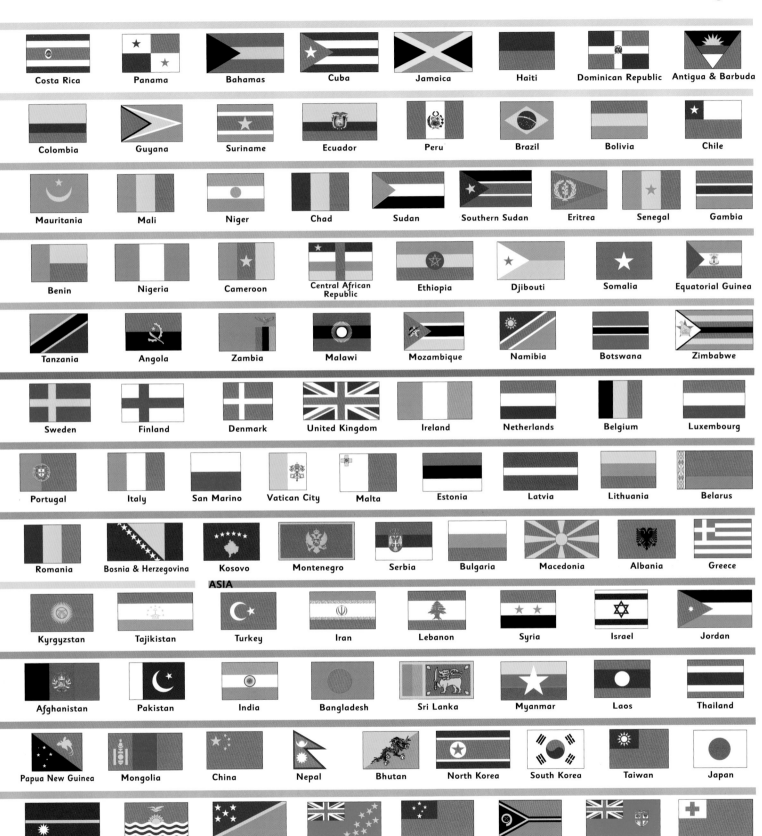

Costa Rica · Panama · Bahamas · Cuba · Jamaica · Haiti · Dominican Republic · Antigua & Barbuda

Colombia · Guyana · Suriname · Ecuador · Peru · Brazil · Bolivia · Chile

Mauritania · Mali · Niger · Chad · Sudan · Southern Sudan · Eritrea · Senegal · Gambia

Benin · Nigeria · Cameroon · Central African Republic · Ethiopia · Djibouti · Somalia · Equatorial Guinea

Tanzania · Angola · Zambia · Malawi · Mozambique · Namibia · Botswana · Zimbabwe

Sweden · Finland · Denmark · United Kingdom · Ireland · Netherlands · Belgium · Luxembourg

Portugal · Italy · San Marino · Vatican City · Malta · Estonia · Latvia · Lithuania · Belarus

Romania · Bosnia & Herzegovina · Kosovo · Montenegro · Serbia · Bulgaria · Macedonia · Albania · Greece

ASIA

Kyrgyzstan · Tajikistan · Turkey · Iran · Lebanon · Syria · Israel · Jordan

Afghanistan · Pakistan · India · Bangladesh · Sri Lanka · Myanmar · Laos · Thailand

Papua New Guinea · Mongolia · China · Nepal · Bhutan · North Korea · South Korea · Taiwan · Japan

Nauru · Kiribati · Solomon Islands · Tuvalu · Samoa · Vanuatu · Fiji · Tonga

Index

Reference Section

Acknowledgments

Dorling Kindersley would like to thank:

Andrew O'Brien for additional digital artworks; Chris Bernstein for compiling the index; Lisa Magloff for editorial assistance and proofreading; Abbie Collinson and Sadie Thomas for design assistance; Pilar Morales for DTP assistance; Simon Mumford for DK cartography; Karl Stange, Gemma Woodward, Sarah Mills for DK Picture Library research

Picture credits